the Magnetic BOSS

How to become the leader
no one wants to leave

Linda D. Henman, Ph.D.

This book is dedicated to the Vietnam Prisoners of War
who taught us all that ordinary people
can do extraordinary things
when they believe in a common purpose,
take care of one another,
and keep their sense of humor.

Henman Performance Group
Chesterfield, Missouri
www.henmanperformancegroup.com

Cover Design: Chris Scavotto; www.scavottodesign.com
Interior Design & Production: Elaine Floyd, EFG Publishing. Inc.

FIRST EDITION

ISBN: 1-930500-18-1

10   09   08   07   06   5   4   3   2   1

Published and distributed to the trade by:
EFG Publishing, Inc.
St. Louis, Missouri
www.efgbookmark.com

CONTENTS

CONTENTS

PREFACE

I began this journey in 1978 when I was too green and too naïve to know what I didn't know. Fortunately, through luck, hard work, or both, I was able to overcome my limitation and offer services that apparently improved my clients' conditions. The following pages chronicle this journey, to reflect my research, experiences, and learnings from more than 25 years of coaching and consulting with hundreds of clients for thousands of hours.

In an ideal world, you would devote copious numbers of hours to reading this book cover to cover, never stopping, not even for meals. Nothing could distract you from your quest to learn all that it has to offer new and experienced bosses. However, there's a slight chance you don't live in an ideal world.

In that case, here are some suggestions. Thumb through each chapter to read the gray boxes. These capture the essence of the section and present it in pithy forms. Next, read the summaries at the end of each chapter. These will give you—well, a summary.

Finally, in the event of a boss emergency, find the relevant topic in the index and go directly to the page that explains what you should do. Good luck. You're on your way to becoming the boss no one will want to leave.

—Linda Henman
Linda@henmanperformancegroup.com
www.henmanperformancegroup.com
St. Louis, Missouri
April 10, 2006

CHAPTER 1

YOU'RE THE BOSS: NOW WHAT?

People don't leave jobs; they leave bosses.
—ANONYMOUS

Congratulations. You're the boss. That means that you own the company; you are related to the owner; or someone thought you had the expertise, experience, or potential to be the leader.

One of these applies, or you know something regarding moral turpitude about your boss. However you got here, here you are.

Chances are no one has really prepared you for this job. In college you studied engineering, marketing, accounting, or some other job function. Maybe you even took a course or two in management, but did anyone ever really teach you the skills needed to be the boss? Probably not.

You, like millions of others, are in this position but are not prepared for all the responsibilities that go with it. If you aren't smart, honest, and hardworking, this book won't help. If you are, and you want to learn the requisite skills to make a difference in your life and the lives of your direct reports, the people who report directly to you, it will.

As the Baby Boomers look toward retirement, the Generation Xers are looking forward to filling the leadership roles that will be vacated. However, the next generation of leaders will face unprecedented challenges in the war for talent. As has happened in the past, people will continue to leave bosses, not jobs.

An unhappy employee will leave for a 5% pay increase, but it takes at least a 20% increase to compel a satisfied employee to jump ship.

But when people leave, there will be fewer top performers to fill key positions. The competition for talent will escalate, and only those companies who have hired magnetic bosses will be able to vie in the global marketplace.

Some estimates indicate that in a healthy job market, an unhappy employee will bolt the company for a five percent pay increase, but it will take at least an increase of 20% to compel a satisfied employee to jump ship. A growing economy makes your job tougher because it creates more jobs, leading to more competition for talent.

Although there seems to be universal agreement that people want to be better bosses, the task of determining what that means seems daunting. Perhaps one of the best ways to answer some of the questions that continue to surface is to describe some of the traditional views about leadership, to think about new ways of viewing leadership, and to explain the transition from solo performer to boss. This will form the foundation for you to understand first how to take care of yourself, then how to lead individuals, and then how to lead groups of individuals.

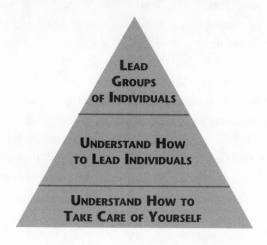

WHAT IS LEADERSHIP?

In 1992 I received one of those dreaded phone calls asking for a parent / teacher conference. I had endured enough of these to know I wasn't going to have fun. When I arrived at the school, the solemn teacher explained that my seven-year-old daughter needed therapy. (I didn't question that, but I wondered how she knew). The teacher related an incident that had happened the day before. It seems that in protest of the cafeteria food, the second graders had decided to bring their lunches from home. Unbeknownst to me, my daughter had chosen to bring dog food.

During lunch she proceeded to eat her lunch of protest. When the other girls asked her what it was, she told them it was dog food. They all squealed the predictable "Ewwww, gross!" She calmly told them that it was better than the cafeteria food, so they all decided to register their complaints by trying it.

The teacher then explained that this incident was why she and the principal had concluded that my daughter needed counseling. I said, "Let me get this straight. Are you telling me that my daughter influenced the entire second-grade class to eat dog food?" She nodded emphatically. I said, "If my seven-year-old daughter can get other kids to eat dog food, I see great leadership potential in her. Please don't squelch it."

She restated, "Well, we think she needs counseling." I inquired whether she could recommend an Alpo 12-Step Program. Their look of disbelief told me they were now concluding that I was the one who needed the help.

Eating dog food is a great metaphor for what leaders do. People don't robotically march off to war and put themselves in harm's way. They don't necessarily want to upset their lives with social reform or political upheaval. They don't automatically champion organizational change that means more work, less stability, or relocation. In its simplest form, leadership is getting others to do what they wouldn't want to do if a leader weren't in the picture. If they would have done it anyway, you're just the person in the front, not the leader. In essence, the leader is the one who gets the other people to eat the dog food.

In essence, the leader is the one who gets the other people to eat the dog food.

However, helping people truly understand what is expected of them as the leader is not quite so simple. Since the beginning of civilization, people have sought answers to the questions of who becomes a leader and why. Philosophers, political scientists, and psychologists have produced extensive literature on leaders and leadership. Despite this, there is still no consensus as to why and under what circumstances some become leaders and others remain followers. Each generation faces new and different variations on the theme.

Not only is there no agreement about a theory of leadership, there are those who question the very notion of leadership. Yet, there has been no indication that leaders are no longer necessary, and apparently there are no successful groups without leaders. Even when some members of a group consciously avoid leader roles, others rise to fill the void. There is no universal theory of leadership, no precise formula for producing leaders, and no definitive answers, even though great minds have wrestled with this question for centuries.

Plato, for example, believed only a select few with superior wisdom should be leaders.

Aristotle contended, "From the moment of their birth, some are marked for subjugation and others for command."

Machiavelli felt that those princes who had the cunning and the ability to organize power and knowledge in the defense of the state should be followed. He believed people are weak, fallible, gullible, and dishonest; therefore, manipulation is acceptable to achieve one's goals when the end justifies the means.

St. Paul said that only those deemed worthy through divine blessing could truly lead. Many believed that God chose leaders through royal or aristocratic birth, and since indeed those men did secure positions of power, the theory seemed credible.

Evidence of more modern theorists feeling the effect of these historical outlooks can be seen in the 1869 publication, *Hereditary Genius*, by Francis Galton, who attempted to explain leadership on the basis of inheritance.

Different forms of this "nature / nurture" controversy continue today. Whether leaders are born with talents and traits that allow and even cause them to be successful leaders, or whether effective leadership behaviors can be learned through experience, is a difficult question. There is not even consensus about universal traits that cause leaders to be effective. Often leaders are intelligent, knowledgeable, attractive, sociable, and persistent; but there are exceptions. There are effective leaders who do not embody one or more of these traits, so defining absolutes is impossible.

From 1920 to 1950 researchers, perhaps feeling the influence of the early trait theorists, tried to pinpoint factors that contribute to effective leadership. They reasoned that if leaders possess superior qualities that differentiate them from followers, discovering these qualities should be possible. They were wrong.

Researchers later identified characteristics such as initiative, social dominance, and persistence as general qualities of effectual leaders, but unfortunately, no common list of specific leadership traits surfaced then either. In fact, researchers not only did not discover a common list of leadership qualities, they also uncovered a number of inconsistent findings.

Their results imply that a person does not become a leader by virtue of the possession of some combination of traits, but the pattern of personal characteristics of the leader must bear some relevant relationship to the characteristics, activities, and goals of the followers. In other words, traits considered singly hold little diagnostic or predictive significance. In combination, however, they can generate personality *dynamics*, or patterns, rather than specific *traits* that are advantageous to the person in a leadership role.

The *situational approach*, which began in the 1960s, on the other hand, denied the influences of differences, attributing all variance among people to fortuitous demands of the environment.

> *There is no right or wrong way to lead all of the time. Matching leaders and groups who meet each other's needs and skills is advised.*

While early trait theorists gave little attention to determining what role the situation might play in leadership requirements, this controversy would receive more attention later as these situational theories evolved. The basis of these theories is that individuals' characteristics make them suitable leaders only in certain situations. Since each situation requires a leader to vary behavior to fit the prevailing circumstances, companies do well to match the leader to the present state of affairs.

In other words, according to these theorists, there is no right or wrong way to lead all of the time. Rather, matching leaders and groups who meet each other's needs and skills is advised. From this standpoint, matching your leadership style to the needs of your direct reports is a good idea.

Take Wally for example. Wally, whose direct reports represented a wide range of abilities, characteristics, experiences, and traits, was a supervisor in a federal government agency. Sheldon, one of those direct reports, was a high-energy go-getter who needed very little direction. Wally merely had to mention an idea, and Sheldon was off and running.

In Sheldon's words, "Wally 'suggested' an activity that he wanted accomplished and discussed desired outcomes. He never told me how to do the activity or established timelines, and he was always open to alternative outcomes. My creative juices got going and my performance was never better than when I was working for Wally."

Others who worked for Wally needed more guidance. They wanted to know what specific tasks he wanted them to accomplish as well as timelines for doing them. Wally realized this and was very flexible in how he managed. He could either be a taskmaster or a visionary as the need arose. Wally had probably not studied situational leadership theorists, but he arrived at their truth through insight and experience. He understood that no one style of leadership works for all of the people all of the time, so he adapted his behavior to match the specific needs of his direct report.

Other theorists, the behaviorists, argued that leadership is learned behavior influenced by genetics but not by the existence of spirits within the body. They contended that the reinforcement of leadership behaviors and punishment, or nonreinforcement of nonleadership behaviors determine who will become a leader.

Although this approach is generally not popular outside a narrow sphere, many theorists still maintain that actions, such as leadership behaviors, can be explained and controlled purely by manipulation of the environment. In their opinion, it follows that if these leadership behaviors can be identified, they can be taught and learned, a direct challenge to the notion that leaders are born, not made. However, another question surfaces: Can leadership be taught only to those who already possess the innate ability to lead?

The first page of this chapter said that if you aren't smart, honest, and hardworking, this book won't help. I'll go a step further. If you don't have these characteristics by the time you apply for a leadership position, no amount of training and coaching will create these for you.

These are what might be considered minimum competencies. You can learn to be better in math, and you can take some classes in logic, but if you don't possess the intellectual horsepower that it takes to do the job, however that is defined in your world, you won't succeed. You certainly can hone leadership skills and learn management functions, but the foundation has to be there.

LEADERS, LEADERSHIP & MANAGEMENT

Some of the confusion and disagreement about leadership can be traced to a failure to distinguish between "the leader" and "leadership." If nothing else, twentieth century social science research has established that leadership is a function of group process, rather than a series of traits residing in a particular individual. Clearly, there is no such thing as a "leader" apart from some particular group. Leaders must have followers. Then, is the impact or effectiveness of the leader measured by the success of the followers? Certainly there are those who would immediately answer "yes!" Losing coaches get fired; CEOs of nonprofitable companies are terminated; and political candidates who make a poor showing at the polls are not elected. But in each of these cases does the failure of the group imply that leadership did not take place?

Who would say that Robert E. Lee did not lead the Confederate forces? Are there those who would accuse Napoleon of not leading his men at Waterloo? Would anyone argue that Hitler did not lead his troops and come dangerously close to realizing his goal? In each of these examples the followers failed. Lee, Napoleon, and Hitler were leaders of losing teams, but the history books still hail them as some of the most influential leaders of all time.

Have the criteria for measuring great leadership changed? Is leadership now defined solely by success? Perceptions and definitions do change with time, and perhaps there is a tendency today to measure success of the leader only by the accomplishments of the group. Certainly, the boss's success will be measured by the accomplishments of those who report to him or her.

> *For the purpose of this discussion, both leader and manager will mean the boss.*

Another confusing question concerns differentiating between leadership and management. In recent years attention has been given to the issue of whether leadership or management is needed in the organization. The obvious question, then, is what is the difference between the two? Definitions differ depending on the author or the theorist, but some common criteria seem to exist for distinguishing between them. Often the duties or responsibilities of managers are delineated. They are concrete, measurable, and observable. This makes defining what managers are and what they do somewhat easier than describing leaders or leadership. Frequently leaders perform all of the practical functions a manager would, but there seems to be an added ingredient.

There is a mystique about leaders. The definitions of leadership involve abstract words such as *visionary, charismatic, proactive,* and *purposeful.* Since these terms are nebulous, putting leadership in specific, observable terms is difficult; and a definition becomes elusive. There is often an emotional reaction to the word "leader." Some might say the distinction is

"Management is doing things right; leadership is doing the right things." It could also be said that leaders inspire others to greater effort, and managers provide the necessary resources for that greater effort. Ideally, would the same person do both, allowing the inspiration and practical application to work in tandem?

Can an effective leader lack practical managerial skills? One possible answer is that all leaders are managers, but not all managers are leaders. The lines between management and leadership are fuzzy because personal connotations overpower objective denotations. Although some real differences do exist in the perceptions of the two terms, for the purpose of this discussion, the two will be used interchangeably; both will mean the boss, and both will imply that the person has power in the organization and has direct reports.

A NEW MODEL OF LEADERSHIP: F^2 LEADERSHIP

Specifically, what does it take to be a good boss? The short answer is it takes a strong bias for action and a keen eye on the people issues.

The constant realigning of these two concerns is the basis of F^2 Leadership, equal parts of fairness and firmness, the cornerstones of effectiveness. F^2 Leadership requires:

- ❑ the ability to do what needs to be done, when it needs to be done, whether or not you want to do it.
- ❑ a desire to lead
- ❑ the intelligence to learn quickly
- ❑ the analytical reasoning to solve unfamiliar, complex problems
- ❑ a strong action orientation
- ❑ integrity
- ❑ people skills

With the exception of people skills, most of these are resistant to change and difficult to develop. The good news is, often leadership derailment is caused by flawed interpersonal skills, so bosses who possess the other characteristics can learn the one set of skills that is likely to have the greatest impact on their success. Therefore, becoming a firm but fair leader that others trust is at the heart of sustaining effective leadership.

F² LEADERSHIP MODEL

FAIRNESS   FIRMNESS

One of the toughest aspects of developing better interpersonal skills is the tricky balance leaders need to have for concern for people and concern for results. Without a strong bias for action, you won't be successful. Effective leadership demands dominance, the exercising of control or influence. It means being assertive, putting forth ideas, and striving to influence the way others turn ideas into action. Dominant leaders take charge, guiding, leading, persuading, and moving other people to achieve results. Instead of *letting* things happen, they *make* things happen. Your success is tied to results, not popularity or providing people a place to go during the day.

Without a strong concern for the people who get the results, however, bosses aren't effective either. Balancing dominance and responsiveness requires constant recalibration, a challenge that even the most seasoned leaders face. Your direct reports don't necessarily have to like you to stay with you, but they will need to respect you as their leader. Here are some ideas for being an F² Leader, one who gets results while still being responsive to others:

- ❑ Demand results through involvement. Set tough goals and insist on analytical approaches.
- ❑ Get to know your people, their strengths, their weaknesses, and their motivators, and then deal with each person as a unique individual.
- ❑ Maintain an "us centered" mentality.
- ❑ Demonstrate concern and responsiveness. Rather than merely trying to please direct reports for the moment,

work with them to uncover their concerns and then balance these with the needs of the organization.

❑ Put disagreements and problems on the table as soon as you perceive them. Don't wait until you are angry or until a crisis is brewing to talk about things.

Sustaining a dedication to excellent results and a commitment to your people will be a huge step toward building trust, an essential component of F^2 Leadership. Although personal integrity is essential for building a trusting, trustworthy organization, it isn't enough. Developing *behaviors* that indicate the integrity is there is also crucial. Like interpersonal skills, the behaviors can be taught and learned, even if the integrity upon which they are based is not easily changed.

Building trust within an organization is a complicated and fragile process that requires the unwavering attention of the leaders at all levels of the organization. Employees need to have trust in the people who are running the organization. They have to believe that decision makers have the vision and competence to set the right course, allocate resources intelligently, fulfill the mission, and help the company succeed. They want to feel confident that processes are well designed, consistent, and fair.

Does the company make good on its promises? Research demonstrates there are links between trust and corporate performance, and common sense indicates, all other things being equal, people will stay with the trusted leader.

Just as important, employees want to trust their own bosses. When determining whether their boss is worthy of their personal trust, direct reports will ask, "Does the boss treat employees fairly? Does she consider her direct reports' needs when making decisions about the business and put the company's needs ahead of her own desires?" If they can't answer "yes" to both questions, there is no foundation on which to build trust.

But what can a boss actually do to build this climate of trust that characterizes F^2 Leadership? Obviously some aspect of trust, like organizational trust, might be outside the purview of a particular leader, but there are many aspects the boss can control:

❑ ***Send consistent messages***. One of the fastest moving destroyers of trust, inconsistent messages, can occur at any level of the organization. Often bosses are helpless to do anything about the strategic or organizational trust issues in their companies, but they can certainly make sure that they are not guilty of sending mixed or inconsistent messages. An element of trust is predictability. Direct reports want to know they can trust their bosses to do what they say they will. For instance, the boss who tells her direct reports how much she values them and then doesn't keep scheduled appointments with them, takes calls or other interruptions when they are meeting, or shows up late for meetings with them, is sending the message loud and clear that indeed they are not important to her. Employees who have this kind of boss can be counted on to disengage, focus on rumors and politics, and update their résumés.

❑ *Keep policies and standards consistent.* When bosses play favorites and allow a few pet performers to bend the rules, others notice. If it's not important enough to have a company policy about, don't bother with it. The "hot stove" form of leadership applies here. No matter who touches the stove, it's hot, and the person touching it will get burned, no matter the person's position in the organization or the favor the boss feels for the person who touches it.

❑ *Don't create a policy in response to the bad behavior of a few.* Don't have a policy about something unless you are willing to fire your most valuable employee for violating it. If you have a direct report that doesn't come to work on time, address the issue with that person instead of instituting an expensive clocking in system that will just annoy others who never needed it in the first place.

❑ *Expect competence, high-quality performance, and decent behavior from everyone.* Whether the person is a genius, technical expert, top salesperson, rainmaker, or company curmudgeon, the same standards should apply, but often they don't. Top performers often get away with volatile behavior and tantrums. The under-performer can also get away with unacceptable behavior simply because bosses don't want the confrontation that is likely to occur if they address issues. Others notice, and they resent the company tolerating problematic employees.

❑ *Give honest, balanced feedback.* Many times I have had conversations with human resource managers frustrated because obviously a person needs to be fired, but the performance reviews are glowing. A legitimate question a lawyer would ask in a wrongful termination hearing might be, "If this employee is bad enough to fire, how do you explain these high scores on his last appraisal?" In addition to causing headaches for the company, this kind of dishonest feedback fails to help the direct report develop skills or take actions to better performance. Similarly, if everyone is given the same bonus and raises, what is the incentive for others to work hard for stellar performance? Motivation may come from within, but *de*motivation often comes from the boss. People tend to object to unfair treatment that they can't control. The boss who engages in flawed feedback is inviting others to weigh in by voting with their feet as they walk out the door.

> *Motivation may come from within, but DEmotivation often comes from the boss.*

❑ *Trust others*. One of the phenomena of human behavior is that trustworthy people are also usually trusting people. As the saying goes, a man only looks behind a door if he has hidden behind several himself. If a boss can't trust his direct reports, one of two things is wrong. Either he is not willing to trust because of his own doubts, or the direct report has given him reason not to trust her.

For example, I worked with Mike, a vice president who routinely worked a 70-hour week. He complained that he had no life balance, and his wife was tired of shouldering all the family responsibilities herself. When I probed more, I learned some of the reasons he was working so many hours on a consistent basis. He failed to delegate because he wanted to ensure quality. Therefore, in addition to all the things he had to do to fulfill his obligations, he reviewed expense accounts to make sure no one was cheating.

These are two separate issues, but both are related to trust. First, Mike needed to let his direct reports know that he trusted them to do their jobs their ways, without his micromanagement. Second, Mike needed to let them know that he expected integrity in their expense accounting. One of his direct reports had previously cheated by taking his wife to dinner on the company. This sort of violation should result in the direct report being punished with either a stern, formal reprimand or dismissal. Mike should not be punished by having to assume the additional duties of reviewing all expenses. This is something one of his direct reports, possibly his assistant, could do.

The ability to foster trust is probably one of the single most important skills an F² Leader needs to develop because it is at the heart of accomplishing tasks and taking care of people. If your direct reports trust you and know that you trust them, they will work to get the results everyone needs for success. What you do to balance task and people issues is your first concern as a boss, but the way you lead will be important too.

IT TAKES STYLE TO BE A GOOD BOSS

Leadership *style*, more than any particular leadership trait, determines leader effectiveness. Style is related to one's model of organizational behavior. The leader's style or manner of dealing with the organization's members and communicating with them contributes to or detracts from the group's overall functioning. Researchers Kurt Lewin and Rensis Likert identified three general approaches to these interactions: *authoritative* leadership style, *democratic* or *participative* leadership style, and *laissez-faire* leadership style.

AUTHORITATIVE LEADERSHIP

Authoritative, or autocratic, leadership relies on legitimate, coercive, and reward power to influence others. Often these kinds of leaders are aggressive, parental, and dictatorial in their dealings with the group. While these approaches often work well in crisis situations, a constant reliance of this style can cause followers to be apathetic and unproductive when the leader's back is turned.

When you constantly use authoritative leadership, the group members fail to develop a sense of ownership of their work. They will work if they are watched, but perhaps since they do not feel a part of the decision- making process, they are not motivated to do more than absolutely necessary. Also, they may become accustomed to the parental guidance of an autocratic leader and rely on it for motivation.

Authoritative or autocratic leadership usually represents an imbalance in F^2 Leadership, with firmness outweighing fairness. However, there are exceptions. During a crisis, others want and need more firmness. When the enemy is advancing over the hill, the platoon sergeant shouldn't call a meeting to hear the concerns of his direct reports. It wouldn't work, and people would get killed. In your world, which might be a corporate battlefield of sorts, therefore, it is appropriate to the situation for you to be more direct when calamity strikes. But keep this in mind: By definition, emergencies happen infrequently. If they happen all the time, they are the way you do business, not crises.

Leonard Schaeffer found that he needed to use an autocratic style when he initially took the reins as CEO at Blue Cross. As Schaeffer learned, in a turnaround situation, a business often needs to change relatively quickly. In these kinds of situations, just making a decision and getting people moving is critical. Schaeffer likened the leader's behavior to that of an emergency room surgeon who is forced to do whatever it takes to save a patient's life. However, as Schaeffer learned, autocracy often causes pain and arouses antagonism. There is no way for the chief executive to escape the resentment and blame that others will direct toward him or her.

The best the CEO can do to mitigate the problem is to assume personal responsibility, act quickly, and stay focused on the most critical issues. Although this is a more pronounced degree of firmness as it relates to F^2 Leadership, if it is appropriate and in the best interest of the organization and the people within the organization, it is what the leaders should do.

DEMOCRATIC LEADERSHIP

FAIRNESS   FIRMNESS

Democratic, or participative, leadership, on the other hand, is usually a closer description of F² Leadership. As the name implies, when this kind of leadership is being practiced, all those affected have a share in the decision-making process. The research indicates that direct reports tend to be more satisfied and less frustrated when they play a part in the group's functioning. Sometimes the boss will still make the final decision after consulting the group members, but generally people feel more validated if their ideas are considered; and they are usually more motivated to implement the decision, even if it doesn't reflect their own input. Bosses who embrace democratic leadership soon learn that groups tend to take longer than individuals to reach a decision, but as a rule, the quality of the decision is better; and the higher morale of the stakeholders has its own rewards.

LAISSEZ-FAIRE LEADERSHIP

Laissez-faire leaders often represent an exaggerated emphasis on fairness, sometimes at the expense of results. These kinds of bosses exert little or no influence on their direct reports. In essence, these groups are a collection of equals. In fact, some would argue that these groups do not have leaders. This kind of leadership can work if the direct reports are capable and driven; however, it can fail if they are unmotivated or inexperienced with the task. An alternative to laissez-faire leadership is "loose-tight" management. Under this kind of management, development of goals, budgets, and strategies is strictly controlled from the top, while direct reports have free rein about how they achieve these objectives, as long as they stay on budget, meet deadlines, and adhere to organizational and industry protocols. This can be considered F² Leadership as long as it is appropriate to the circumstances and the individuals involved.

Democratic leadership is usually considered the best of the styles, but no one style is indicated all of the time. Democratic leadership works well when nonstressful, moderate conditions prevail, but autocratic leadership is more suitable during a crisis or high stress situation. Even the laissez-faire style can work well if the group is self-directed and motivated.

The successful F² Leader is one who can adapt to the unique demands of an ever-changing organization. An effective leader needs to diagnose the needs and wants of followers and then react accordingly, remembering all the while that the group is becoming more experienced and less dependent on direction. Recognizing the power that the leader has and the power that the group members share helps leaders and followers more effectively share the leadership functions and contribute to overall productivity.

Defining and explaining leadership are monumental tasks. Lessons from psychology, history, sociology, religion, and business are just a few of the things that should be considered when approaching this topic; and yet it is still overwhelming. The search for answers goes on, and the questions continue to change. Plato, Aristotle, Machiavelli, and St. Paul might not agree with current theories, but given the challenges of running a twenty-first century organization, they would probably be faced with the need to re-examine some of their thinking.

TRANSITIONING FROM SOLO CONTRIBUTOR TO BOSS

As leaders throughout history have learned, the first 90 days in a position are critical. If these days have passed and you didn't take advantage of them, it's not too late to start doing some of the basics, no matter where you are in your leadership progression. However, if you haven't yet weathered the first three months of your job, think about the top five things you can do to launch you as a boss that others will respect and not want to leave.

1. *First, talk to your new boss*. Find out what expectations she or he has in mind for you. Discuss your own goals and aspirations for the job. Write it all down. Keep a copy for yourself and give one to your boss. Make sure the goals are realistic but ambitious. If you aren't certain what your boss expects, it's highly unlikely that you'll deliver. If you don't know what decisions you should be making and which ones you should be getting help with, ask

about that too. There's no such thing as too much information during these first three months. Most bosses aren't particularly good at coaching their direct reports, so you might have to pull the coaching out of them.

2. ***Talk to the people who report directly to you***. Mirror the discussion you had with your own boss. Make sure that you and they know what you expect and find out what they need from you to get results. Remember, they are more nervous about having you as a boss than you are about being one. Communication is the only way to ameliorate the tensions.

3. ***When appropriate, talk to clients or customers***. What do they appreciate that they want you to continue to deliver? What do they see as areas needing improvement? Giving them what they want is the key to your success, so don't be tempted to overlook these conversations.

4. ***Find a mentor who is not your boss***. Reams of evidence exist to support the conclusion that help from others is significant. The trouble is, you're probably an independent sort who is where you are because you are self-reliant and resourceful. That worked then; other things work now. You are sailing in uncharted seas now that you have a new job, so you will need to benefit from the sage advice of those who have gone before you. The mentor can be a person in the organization who is more senior, or the mentor can be someone outside the company whose advice you value. Usually, just inviting the person to have lunch with you once a month will be flattering enough for most to accept. (By the way, you should pick up the check!)

5. ***Read. Read anything and everything***. Certainly you should read a daily newspaper and the industry periodicals. But you should also read a news magazine and the Wall Street Journal. If your city has a weekly business journal, read that too. At any given time, you should have read at least two books on the best seller list. In addition to giving you valuable information, this reading will make you a more interesting person. When I meet successful executives, I am constantly amazed at the sheer volume of their reading. No matter what subject comes up, they have read a little about it. Successful executives also read challenging novels for pleasure. How do they find the time? They don't watch much television, and they protectively guard their leisure time.

There are many business books on the shelves that offer advice about the 10 traps of leaders or the five mistakes leaders make in their first 90 days, but I find that most of life comes down to three simple rules, my personal credo. In fact, the previous five suggestions for your first months in office could come under one of these headings:

- ❑ *Never run out of altitude, airspeed, and ideas at the same time.* Chapter Six will give you more specifics about this, but in a nutshell, it means you have to make good decisions, keep a global perspective, build relationships, and be flexible. The rest can be taken care of in rule two. Pilots of a supersonic aircraft may run out of one, but if they run out of all three at the same time, they are given the dubious distinction of occupying a place of honor at some national cemetery. As the boss, if you run out of all three at the same time, you will be given a less than ceremonial burial.

- ❑ *If what you're doing is not working, quit doing it and do something else.* I'm constantly amazed that otherwise sane people continue on a path that has never led to anything but disappointment. If you keep doing what you've always done, you'll get the results you've always gotten. It's really quite simple.

- ❑ *Don't annoy crazy people.* The previous two rules cover most of life's challenges, but this one needs to be articulated. No good comes of annoying crazy people; it bothers them and frustrates you.

In addition to all these ideas for transitioning from solo performer to boss, there is one other important issue. In order to be effective, leaders must have a desire to lead. Even if an individual has the talent and training to lead but no motivation to work for a leadership position, success is unlikely. Sometimes a desire for popularity or a wish to avoid stress and responsibility causes an individual to seek nonleadership roles. Certainly there are people who pass up promotions for various reasons. Often such people are more motivated by needs that have nothing to do with the need for recognition, which is often satisfied by acquiring a leadership role.

For example, Scott was a client who had been a top-notch, energetic go-getter in a technology company. His stellar performance in every job he had filled since joining the company right out of college caused the leadership to think of him as a fast mover. The more responsibility they gave him, the more he rose to the challenge. He was smart, motivated, talented, and strategic. He loved the

> *Exceptional individual performance does not guarantee great leadership performance.*

feelings of achievement that he got from a job well done. What he didn't love was the feeling of vulnerability that comes from counting on others to do the work that will determine a successful outcome. Scott came to me to learn "leadership skills," a goal that shouldn't be too difficult to achieve, given his intellectual capacity and success orientation. But Scott lacked something, the very thing that would stand in his way up the ladder.

After evaluating Scott and interviewing him, I finally asked, "Are you sure you are ready to have your success depend on the accomplishments of others?" He didn't hesitate very long before he said, "That just scares the hell out of me, Linda." In short, Scott seemed to be echoing Bill Cosby's sentiments when he talked about not being the boss of his family. Cosby concluded, as did Scott, that he had seen the boss's job, and he didn't want it.

Scott's attitude might have cost him professionally if he had been in an "up or out" kind of organization, but this particular company had room for strong solo performers. This isn't always the case, but when it is, decision makers do well to realize that not all people want to be the boss. When this happens, avoiding the temptation to put people in jobs for which they are not suited will pay off in the long run.

But what about the strong solo performer who does want to transition to being the boss? This isn't such an easy proposition either. Exceptional individual performance does not guarantee great leadership performance. Leadership is a relationship, a reciprocal process that is person-dependent. Transitioning into it demands that the person learn ways to use people skills to engage others, all the while keeping values and beliefs engaged and standards of performance high. Transitioning also depends on you learning some behaviors to help you help others make you and them more successful. I hope this book helps.

SUMMARY

After all this discussion, a question does begin to surface:

What role does chance or luck play in the rise of a leader?

Would Hitler, for example, have been able to wreak such formidable havoc had he been at a different place lived in a different time? From all this, you might infer that timing has a lot to do with the outcome of a rain dance and leadership.

However, understanding more about how to become the boss that no one wants to leave begins with an understanding of what a boss is. Then, each person must ask the tough question, "Do I really want to be the boss?"

Finally, the person who steps up to the plate needs to know how to do what it takes to succeed. Only after you have this foundation can you begin the formidable task of learning what needs to be done to win. Specifically, this journey will require:

1. Some skills related to taking care of oneself

2. Some abilities to lead each individual

3. A grasp of what it takes to lead a group of people—either a team of direct reports or an entire organization

The principles are the same, even though they are not easy to practice at any level. But what worthwhile things are easy?

As Winston Churchill pointed out, "Success is not final, failure is not fatal; it is the courage to continue that counts."

And as Tom Hank's character said in *A League of Their Own*, "If it were easy, anyone could do it."

CHAPTER 2

MAKE PEOPLE **GLAD** YOU'RE THEIR BOSS

Leadership is lifting a person's vision to higher sights,
the raising of a person's performance to a higher standard,
the building of a personality beyond its normal limitations.
—PETER DRUCKER

People won't leave if they're glad you're their boss. They will want to stay with a boss who knows them and does what it takes to create a culture that capitalizes on each individual's strength.

Often bosses don't know what they should do to contribute to organizational culture, or even to their small part of the culture. For so long, people have tried to diagnose diseases, flaws, and weaknesses, but most of us have had precious little experience studying health. However, knowing more about healthy people enables us to understand resilience and hardiness, the cornerstones required for building something— something like a solid relationship with direct reports.

Learning ways to more effectively interact with those who work for you and challenging yourself to discover their strengths so that you can do your part to motivate them are enormous steps toward realizing the goal of being a boss that no one wants to leave.

DEVELOP A **GLAD** CULTURE

Without seeing the inherent flaws in their thinking, many bosses worry overmuch about what they *say* to their direct reports. Certainly sending effective messages is important, but developing relationships with others that exemplify the GLAD Communication Method is more critical for creating positive working relationships with direct reports. Seldom do direct reports complain that their bosses don't talk to them enough. Bosses, like many parents, often think they need to develop their people by *talking* to them. It never occurs to them that a more important aspect of developing others is actually *listening* to them.

GLAD is an acronym for the four-step communication method that enables bosses and direct reports to have routine conversations, difficult discussions, and feedback sessions. Bosses who learn and practice this method learn that their modeling this behavior eventually causes others to adopt it too. The outcome is an environment in which employees are GLAD to be there, and so are their bosses.

(G)et to the core of the performance issues.

(L)isten to the other person first.

(A)dd your own ideas.

(D)evelop an action plan.

(G)ET TO THE CORE OF THE ISSUE

Getting to the core of the issue means focusing the discussion on one specific issue. It also means focusing the discussion on *actions* or *behaviors*, things the person can control and change. If personality issues or decision-making capacities are interfering with the person's performance, the problem may be an inability, rather than an unwillingness, to do the job. In that case, the boss needs to consider alternatives either to give the direct report additional help or move him or her to an area that is better suited for that person's talents and strengths.

When giving feedback or holding a difficult discussion, focus on one concern that can be expressed in one sentence. If it won't fit into one sentence, it is more than one discussion. If you try to lump too many things together, the direct report will leave confused and frustrated.

Start the discussion with "The problem is...." Be sure to express the problem in *concrete, observable, descriptive* terms.

The problem is _____

To help you determine if you have clear language, ask yourself these questions:

❑ If I were following the person around, what would I see? Hear?
❑ What does the direct report need to start doing? Stop doing? Do differently?
❑ If this were fixed, how would I know?

Bosses are often tempted to center the discussion around the *symptoms* of the problem instead of on the actual problem. For example, a grocery store manager told me his direct report just "didn't communicate with his direct reports enough." I asked how he knew. In other words, where was the pain? He said turnover was high; shrink was high; and costs were high. I pointed out that he had just described three problems that may or may not have anything to do with the man in question communicating to his direct reports.

> *If you discipline yourself to talk about facts and commit to listening first, the likelihood of solving problems skyrockets.*

When forced to separate the causes from effects and unrelated issues from each other, he was able to get his hands around exactly what he needed to coach his employee about. Once this was apparent, the boss was able to clearly articulate the problem that was costing them the most: "The problem is turnover is costing the store X dollars per year, an increase in X dollars from this time last year." The direct report knew exactly what the issue was and was able to address strategies for improvement.

Contrast this scenario to the boss beginning with the statement, "You don't communicate with your people enough." It's very likely that the direct report would think or say, "I communicate plenty." If the boss and the direct report don't even agree on what the problem is, there's very little chance that they will be able to solve the problem.

On the other hand, if the boss makes a statement of fact that plainly describes the tangible consequences, there can be little room for disagreement, at least during this step. Often this statement of fact will describe the pain or consequences of an action, usually in their simplest terms. If you discipline yourself to talk about facts and commit to listening first, the likelihood of solving problems skyrockets.

(L)ISTEN TO OTHERS FIRST

If you're like most bosses, when someone comes to you with a problem, you try to be responsive and jump in to fix things for your direct report. Solving problems is what you're all about, so it comes easily and naturally. Plus, it just feels like the right thing to do, and it saves time. However well intended you might be, you are inadvertently passing up a chance to develop rapport with and abilities in the direct report.

Listening first has many advantages. First, you will show your concern and responsiveness by patiently allowing the other to explain the issue. Second, you will operate from a basis of factual knowledge, not guesswork or probability. Third, you will have more of a chance of understanding the whole picture, not just a segment of it.

Stephen Covey called this seeking "first to understand," a step that comes before seeking to be understood. People will understand you better if you show them that you have taken the time to understand them first. Often caring, compassionate bosses are shocked when their 360 degree, multi-feedback data indicate that other people don't always know that they care about them. More often than not, in fact, these 360 data show that direct reports don't feel that the boss is listening to them, much less understanding them.

Listening is one of the skills that otherwise effective leaders often need to develop or hone. However, taking the time to listen patiently to others does not always have immediate payoffs. In an attempt to move projects ahead more efficiently, the boss overlooks opportunities to hear what their direct reports have to say.

Listening to the other person first shows a willingness to consider new information, and if necessary, to change the nature of the discussion. Similarly, hearing the other person sets the tone for the give-and-take that will be necessary to create understanding and commitment between the two. To improve listening, consider these four steps:

1. *Listen first before you give your own ideas*. Listen to understand, not judge.

2. *Don't interrupt*. When people are on a roll, just listen without saying a word. You can show you are listening by saying the occasional, "Oh?" but usually once people have started, they don't

need too much encouragement. You can communicate your receptivity nonverbally by leaning forward, maintaining direct eye contact, closing your door, and putting your phone on mute, but words are usually unnecessary. Of course, you should avoid gestures such as folded arms, looking away, yawning, or playing with objects on the desk, but other than the obvious, there isn't anything you have to do except listen and take notes, if the situation indicates that you should.

3. *Summarize and paraphrase*. Restate facts and reflect emotions that may interfere with the rest of the conversation. Paraphrasing is not parroting, however. It is a restatement of what you heard. For example, if a direct report comes to you with a problem that involves her not knowing which of two alternatives she should choose, you might say, "Well, it seems that you have two alternatives, but neither seems like the right answer, and you aren't too crazy about either one." This will give her a chance to reflect on her statements and to clarify for you, and perhaps herself, what she thinks is the best course of action. The trick is to concentrate on responding nondefensively when people express viewpoints that are contrary to your own.

4. *Ask at least two open-ended questions*. Take advantage of the opportunity to address as many issues as possible with open questions. Asking the employees to talk about their perceptions of problem areas will reduce the defensive reaction that can accompany the boss giving a solution. Ask at least two open, clarifying "How?" "What?" questions to deepen your understanding and to give you all the pertinent information. For example, I once asked a client, Rick, "What feedback have you given your direct report about this?" Rick, the president of his division, had an epiphany from the question. His face lit up as he answered, "I know, Linda. I should be giving Brian more feedback about what he's doing that I don't like." I then asked, "How do you think Brian would react if he knew you felt this way?" He said, "Well, knowing what a go-getter Brian is, he'd be all over this. I know. I have nothing to lose." I hadn't given one word of advice. I had just listened to Rick and asked him two open-ended questions that allowed him to discover his own answers. My goal

when I coach clients is the same goal that bosses have. I want to help them develop their own skills so that they won't need me anymore.

At this point, a common reaction is, "This will take so long! I don't have time to ask a lot of questions. It's so much faster to just tell people the problem and tell them how to fix it."

That's true. The most economical use of time, at least in the short run, is to tell people what to do to fix things. But that sort of behavior leads to other problems. Sometimes people resist being told what to do; the boss doesn't give the employee the chance to discover solutions; and direct reports become reliant on the boss for decisions they should be making themselves. One way or the other, if you persist in jumping in to fix things for others, you will end up annoyed.

> As the boss, you are going to encounter many opportunities to keep your mouth shut. Take advantage of at least some of them.

The behaviors outlined in this chapter will help you *show* you are a better listener, but to truly be one, you will need to adjust your listening habits and attitudes. Opening your mind to really *hear* the message is key. Listening for facts and ideas is important, but that is only part of the picture. Emotions are important too. I have often said, only partially facetiously, that if every boss in America would follow these simple four steps to better listening, the economy would improve overnight.

We know that listening is not the absence of talking; it is the presence of attention. It does not mean simply maintaining a polite silence while you are rehearsing in your mind what you will say the next time there is the slightest lull in the discussion. Nor does listening mean patiently waiting for flaws to appear in someone's arguments so that later you can annihilate him or her.

Listening is not simply hearing; it is comprehension; it is the art of total involvement. It requires participation, action, and effort. It is the glue that holds conversations together and the foundation of understanding. Effective listening skills can be learned; however, like all communication skills, listening requires practice and technique. As the boss, you are going to encounter many opportunities to keep your mouth shut. Take advantage of at least some of them.

(A)DD YOUR OWN IDEAS

Listening to the other first doesn't mean the boss should not give direction. On the contrary, the third step, to add your own ideas, is the time to do just that. Ideally the discussion to this point should have implied a course of action for the direct report. If, in spite of your best efforts, that hasn't happened, the third step is the time to give that direction.

Once again, clearly defining the specific behaviors the direct report should address will help to keep the discussion focused. If the boss disagrees with the employee's assessment of the situation, if there has been a shift in priorities, or if the two disagree on action steps, this is the time for the boss to express ideas and concerns and to begin a discussion about how to resolve differences.

The direct report needs to have a clear understanding of what you expect, those things the employee needs to do more of or less of to improve. Be sure to communicate the "why" behind the "what." Compliment efforts the direct report has made to move projects forward and offer suggestions when people seem stuck. However, communicate clearly that *results* matter. In other words, effective feedback concentrates on what the direct report has *accomplished* not what he or she spent time *attempting* to accomplish.

(D)EVELOP A PLAN OF ACTION

After clearly defining the problem, listening to the other person first, and adding your own ideas, you and your direct report are ready to answer the all-important question, "So what?" What needs to happen now to rectify the problem and move ideas to fruition? An action plan, the agreement you reach with your direct reports, is a way to ensure that you and they agree to the next steps. It captures the essence of the conversation and holds people accountable to deliver on their commitments. The action plan is a fluid document that should change with new information, accomplishments, unexpected events, and learning. To make the most of the action planning step, working together, you and your direct reports need to prioritize goals and objectives to identify the two current most important action items. More than two action items will jeopardize the direct report's efforts to accomplish anything. There can be an unlimited number of "how's" to the two "what's," however.

Timelines for goals help this process. Sometimes the timeline will be obvious. At other times, timelines will need to be created, often in response to new initiatives or demands. Some people have the capacity to break large projects into manageable parts; others need direction from the boss to do so. The main payoff of the action plan is not the form or the document but the discussion. Once the employee and you know what is needed and expected, each has identified roadblocks, and the timeline is clear, the action plan is apparent.

This does not imply that writing the action plan is optional. A written action plan is the tangible agreement among the stakeholders. It serves as a kind of report card for tracking results and redirecting efforts. Therefore, both the boss and the direct report should keep a copy of the original agreement and the subsequent notes and changes.

KNOW THE PEOPLE WHO REPORT TO YOU

The first step to getting to know the people who report to you is to listen to them, and now you have the step-by-step GLAD Communication Method to do just that. With this basic tool in your toolbox, you will be ready for the more sophisticated applications of it, techniques that equip you to build a culture that allows people to be motivated and productive.

Much has been written about motivation, but the simplest way to know what your direct reports are thinking and feeling is to ask them and listen to their responses. This can and should be done routinely throughout the year, but at least a couple times a year, you should invite your direct reports to give more focused feedback about what they need. These conversations should not occur at the same time that performance appraisals occur, however. This is not you giving your direct report feedback; it's the other way around.

One of the things I recommend is a simple, 10 question format with a 10 point rating scale. This scale allows you to debrief in percentages and makes things pretty clear to both the direct report and you. Once you put this process in place, your direct reports will start to expect the email that asks them to fill out the questionnaire and then schedule an appointment to debrief it. Filling out the questionnaire takes about five minutes, and the debrief takes about an hour. Both you and your direct report will quickly learn that this is a painless, important process.

FEEDBACK FORM FOR DIRECT REPORTS

On a scale from 1-10, with 10 meaning you strongly agree and 1 meaning you strongly disagree, rate the following:

I know what my boss expects of me.	1	2	3	4	5	6	7	8	9	10
I have the resources I need to do my job right.	1	2	3	4	5	6	7	8	9	10
My talents and skills are being utilized to their fullest extent.	1	2	3	4	5	6	7	8	9	10
My work is challenging.	1	2	3	4	5	6	7	8	9	10
If I want, I have the chance to advance in skills.	1	2	3	4	5	6	7	8	9	10
I have the chance to advance in responsibilities and position.	1	2	3	4	5	6	7	8	9	10
My boss gives me recognition and praise when I deserve it.	1	2	3	4	5	6	7	8	9	10
I know that my boss cares about me.	1	2	3	4	5	6	7	8	9	10
I can trust my boss to tell me the truth.	1	2	3	4	5	6	7	8	9	10
This company is committed to excellence.	1	2	3	4	5	6	7	8	9	10

There isn't anything magical about these 10 questions. They are just the vehicles that will drive the discussions that you need to have with your direct reports to get to know them better. When you have the answers to these 10 questions, you will know what you need to do to help each person feel valued and appreciated, feelings that help you improve your coaching of average employees and keep your top talent from walking out the door.

HELP DIRECT REPORTS LEVERAGE
THEIR STRENGTHS

Knowing more about your direct reports and their strengths is the first step to helping them leverage their strengths. In their research, the authors of *Now Discover Your Strengths* found that giving people the opportunity to do what they do best is critical to keeping them productive and engaged. They simply wanted to know the answer to the question, "At work do you have the opportunity to do what you do best every day?"

When employees answered "strongly agree" to this question, they were 50% more likely to work in a business with lower employee turnover, 38% more likely to work in more productive business units, and 44% more likely to work in a business with high customer satisfaction scores. Over time, when these businesses increased the number of employees who strongly agree, they saw a comparable increase in productivity, customer loyalty, and employee retention.

Only about 20% of surveyed employees who are working in large organizations feel that their strengths are in play every day.

In short, learning ways to help your direct reports leverage their strengths more effectively just makes good business sense. Yet, only about 20% of surveyed employees who are working in large organizations feel that their strengths are in play every day. Furthermore, the longer employees stay with an organization and the higher they climb, the less likely they are to feel that they are playing to their strengths.

Companies have only to look inside their four walls to find the wealth of unrealized capacity that resides in every employee. But this takes time, a commitment to the process, listening, and a way for discovering strengths; but quite frankly, bosses are more accustomed to operating under the flawed assumption that they should constantly address problems. Most bosses take their direct reports' assets and skills for granted and focus performance reviews, feedback, and training on minimizing their weaknesses.

One more defect in their thinking is that they legislate work style. Determined to uphold standards, bosses often concentrate on how their direct reports are doing a task rather than on the fact that they are doing it well in their own way. Policies and procedures are often critical factors to consider, but more often allowing people the freedom to choose how they will be productive will ensure that they are.

Following the Platinum, not the Golden, Rule is one opportunity for bosses to help others use their strengths. The Golden Rule says that we should treat others the way we would like to be treated. The Platinum Rule states that you should treat others the way they want to be treated. But the only way you will know how they want to be treated is to ask them and to learn more about them.

> *Malcontents seem to siphon a disproportionate amount of the boss's energy and attention.*

Years ago there was a book written for teachers about a school for animals. In this school, each animal was expected to take all the classes. The gazelle had to take a tree climbing course; the fish had to take running classes; birds had to take swimming instruction. Every animal failed the class that required it to operate outside its normal scope of talent. Instead of teaching fish new and better ways to be stellar water creatures, the school forced them to concentrate on running, tree climbing, and flying. The well-intentioned school board decided that birds could not graduate until they had mastered swimming. No animal was able to graduate since no animal could master all the requisite skills.

Are we so different in corporate America? Instead of appreciating people for who and what they are, don't we continue to try to make them something they are not? Certainly you should challenge people to grow and learn, but why not concentrate on their strengths? I have read nothing that tells me Tiger Woods spends time throwing baseballs so that he can be a better Major League contender. Instead, he uses his training time to become better at the game that he already dominates. Granted, there are parts of his game that are better than others, but he sticks with what he's good at. We know these truths from sports and nature, but we continue to do that which is counter-intuitive in business.

Finally, bosses frequently make the mistake of giving the squeaky wheel all the grease. Troublemakers, average or below average performers, and malcontents seem to siphon a disproportionate amount of the boss's energy and attention. By giving your attention to these direct reports, you are rewarding bad behavior and denying your attention to the ones who deserve it. The high potentials in your group are the ones who will get the job done and take the organization to the next level of success. If you can help these people discover their assets and talents, and if working together, you can coach them to their next level, you will build a boss/direct report relationship that anyone would hate to leave.

MAKE THEM GLAD YOU'RE THE BOSS

SUMMARY

Knowing your people and spotlighting each person's strengths will help you do your part to build an organization that helps people play to their strengths and keep reaching for more ways to consistently deliver perfect or nearly perfect performance.

What will you have to do to make people GLAD you're their boss?

You will need:

1. A strong commitment from you to plan conversations, especially difficult ones.

2. A willingness to get to know your people.

3. An eagerness to help them leverage their strengths.

To accomplish all three:

Get to the core of the issue.

Listen first.

Add your own ideas.

Develop an action plan.

These will go a long way to making them GLAD you're their boss.

Remember, a pat on the back is only a few centimeters from a kick in the pants; it takes no more time to perform; and it can make all the difference in the world.

Your encouragement and direction will help others avoid the trap of setting low personal standards for themselves and then consistently failing to achieve them.

CHAPTER 3

VISIBLE, VIRTUAL, OR VERBAL:
SOLVE COMMUNICATION PROBLEMS

The heart of a fool is in his mouth,
but the mouth of a wise man is in his heart.
—BENJAMIN FRANKLIN

When it comes to bosses talking to their direct reports, talk is cheap, chiefly because supply exceeds demand. As Chapter 2 mentioned, usually your direct reports need for you to listen to them more than you talk to them. However, that doesn't imply that you shouldn't be as committed to effective message *sending* as you are to successful message *receiving*.

Ironically, one of the major problems between bosses and direct reports is that when bosses aren't talking too much, they are often talking too little. When bosses aren't overloading direct reports with too much information, they tend to rely on ESP to send their messages. They expect their direct reports somehow just to *know* what the boss wants of them. The problem is, so many direct reports are not equipped to read your thought waves, even if you are truly adept at sending them. They will actually need for you to *tell* them what your message is. Therefore, striking a balance between communication overload and underload is an essential skill you will need to hone, not as essential as active listening, but important nonetheless.

Even when you put aside ESP and carefully choose your words, the success of communication relies heavily on the participants following certain unwritten rules so that the receiver *decodes* the message in much the same way as you *encoded* it.

Striking a balance between communication overload and underload is an essential skill.

Only then does communication occur. As simple as this process sounds, how often have you said something that you thought was perfectly clear, only to find out later that the receiver had taken it in *exactly* the wrong way? Communication is a complex interaction, primarily because humans are involved; therefore, a boss's ability to communicate well with direct reports depends on several factors: the proficiency to use language successfully, the skill to send congruent verbal and nonverbal messages, and the ability to resolve conflict. When you've mastered these, you have a fighting chance of enjoying clear communication, but realize that it's still only a chance.

PROBLEM #1:
WORDS DON'T MEAN; PEOPLE MEAN

Verbal communication is the creation of meaning between people through the use of words, the tools we need to transmit meaning from one person to the other. Words give us the ability to represent the world through symbols, a skill that allows us to make sense of our world and then to share that meaning with others. Our choice of words helps to shape our reality, and our perception of reality influences our choice of words.

The very words that empower us to create meaning with one another, however, can also create barriers between us because each of us assigns words the meaning we want them to have. The word itself doesn't have a universal meaning, even though millions of pages of dictionaries exist for the sole purpose of helping us develop common reactions to words. Instead, words are our code for transmitting our ideas to others. The trouble is, words are pesky little rascals that can be used in more than one way.

For instance, consider the newspaper headline:

"Safety Experts Say School Bus Passengers Should Be Belted."

I know driving a school bus must be very tiring, but do we really want someone hitting our children? Or, does this imply that the driver should give them all a belt of whiskey? Probably the safety experts were advocating the use of seat belts, but based on the words alone, can we be sure? Intentionally or unintentionally, words can cause roadblocks to understanding.

For example, in an experiment conducted in Britain, people around the world were invited to judge jokes on an Internet site as well as contribute their own. The LaughLab research, carried out by psychologist Dr. Richard Wiseman, from the University of Hertfordshire, attracted more than 40,000 jokes and almost two million ratings. The following joke was the winner:

> *Two hunters are out in the woods when one of them collapses. He doesn't seem to be breathing and his eyes are glazed. The other guy takes out his phone and calls the emergency services.*
>
> *He gasps: "My friend is dead! What can I do?" The operator says: "Calm down. I can help. First, let's make sure he's dead."*
>
> *There is a silence, then a gunshot is heard. Back on the phone, the guy says: "OK, now what?"*

Sometimes the receiver decoding words differently than the sender intended is grist for the humor mill, but these mistakes don't serve us well when we are trying to send a message in earnest.

Words give us the means for sharing ideas and expressing emotion, but they can also serve as barriers. Certainly, the hunter and the emergency service operator experienced a barrier to effective communication. One of the reasons for these barriers is, even though meaning is not in words, we act as though it is. Just because a thought makes perfect sense in our heads doesn't in any way imply that anyone else will understand that idea in exactly the same way that we do.

Words are arbitrary mixtures of letters that represent concepts. Because concepts differ, and because people assign symbols to concepts in different and often unpredictable ways, misunderstandings occur. There are no guarantees that communication will ever occur in the way we intend for it to, but there are some things bosses can do to try to control the direction a conversation goes, and hopefully avoid the fate of the hunter's friend.

Be Receiver Oriented

Most bosses don't set out to offend others in their choices of words, but many do anyway. There is a pervasive frustration about what words should or should not be used, what is currently "politically correct," and how to go about staying current on out-of-favor expressions.

Obviously, any term that demeans a group is not appropriate. Adult females don't want to be called the "girls" at the office, yet one of these women may refer to a "girls' night out" herself. "Handicap" is okay for a discussion of a golf game, but "physically challenged" or "disabled" is more widely preferred otherwise. How is a person to know? Often you won't. There will always be those people who prefer "negative patient outcome" to "death," but how much sense does it make to try to placate everyone, especially when clear communication is compromised?

In some cases, you can simply ask if a person prefers "Doug" to "Douglas." In other situations, you'll need to educate yourself about current thinking. In all situations, common sense should prevail. Calling The Swamp Thing a "wetlands-challenged mutant" won't move clarity too far forward. On the one hand, we need to be sensitive; on the other hand, we can't sanitize our language to the point that we don't understand each other. Fortunately, the use of specific language can help us strike that important balance.

Use Specific Language

First, use *concrete* rather than *abstract* words. Let people understand exactly what you're talking about by using exact, precise language. For

> Abstract words ignore uniqueness or even subtle differences.

instance, if I were to tell you that I have an *organism* growing at my home, what would you infer? That I have a science fair project growing in the refrigerator?

If I were more specific and said I have a *pet*, how does your perception change? Dog? Fish? Turtle? Hamster? Bird? Cat? A picture of one of these might have flashed across your mind's eye, perhaps because you have a pet like one of these. If I then said that I have a *feline*, you probably don't suspect that I own a puma; in all probability you envision a domesticated house cat. If I then said I have a black and gray, long-haired Himalayan, you have a much better idea of the organism that is growing at my house because I used a *concrete* rather than *abstract* term to let you know precisely what I was talking about.

Abstract words are unclear because they are broad in scope. They tend to lump things together, ignoring uniqueness or even subtle differences. Abstract words describe things that cannot be sensed through one of the five senses. Because these words are vague, they encourage generalizations and stereotyping. Some examples of abstract words that bosses tend to use are: *attitude, communication, loyalty, commitment, thorough, high-caliber, improvement*, and *reliable*. Unless your direct reports use these words in the *exact* way that you do, they won't receive your message accurately.

Concrete language, on the other hand, is more specific. Concrete words frequently describe things that can be perceived by using one of the five senses or that can be described in behavioral terms. They clarify the sender's meaning by narrowing the number of possibilities. Using concrete words, therefore, tends to decrease the likelihood of misunderstanding.

For example, I recently worked with the owner of a grocery store chain who had decided that he wanted to give one of his store managers some feedback about the conditions of the stores. I asked him what he would like to see changed, and he said "the environment of the store."

If you send vague messages, good things won't happen. In their eagerness to please you, people will do something different, but not necessarily what you had in mind.

I told him that, in my perception, that meant he wanted the store windows to be clean, the aisles to be clear, and the store, even near the fish counter, to smell nice. I mentioned these things because these are the things I notice first about a grocery store. He said, no, none of those things had occurred to him at all. He was talking about the way they display boxes of merchandise on the shelves. He likes for them to be even on the top. I told him I had honestly never noticed or cared whether the boxes lined up.

Here we were, two native speakers, supposedly speaking the same language, who couldn't understand one another. So, to help him craft a more concrete message, I asked him the pivotal question, "If I were following you into the store, what would I see? Smell? Hear?" This helped him pinpoint what he wanted to say.

Similarly, I often work with bosses who want to talk to a direct report about his attitude or communication style. I ask, "If he changed in ways that you wanted him to, and I were following him around, what change would I notice?" This is the crucial question that will help you make your words more specific and concrete. How do you know if someone has a better attitude? Does he smile more? Say hello to more customers? Come out into the store more often? The more specific you can be, the more likely the other will understand you.

Here's a word of caution. If you engage in inaccurate or vague message sending, good things won't happen. In their eagerness to please you, people will do *something* different, but not necessarily what you had in mind. I had this awakening in a training session, ironically focused on better message sending. I asked the participants to turn to a certain page and then gave them the instructions of what they needed to do in their small groups. Unfortunately, I had neglected to put on my reading glasses before making the assignment, so I read the wrong page. Dutifully they went to the page I had instructed them to go to and attempted to do what I had asked them to do. No one mentioned that my instructions made absolutely no sense. No one called my attention to the fact that I was sending them on an impossible mission.

They worked together for the allotted time and then came together as a large group to debrief. After one or two sentences, I realized that things were not adding up. I asked what they were doing and concluded that they had been on the wrong page, or the right page from the instructions, but the wrong page as far as making sense. Keep in mind that I was not the boss of them; I had absolutely no power over them; and they had no reason whatsoever to be intimidated about asking me for clarification. Still, they didn't. They did what they thought I wanted them to do and wasted valuable time. But it wasn't their fault; it was mine. I had not made sure that I had sent a clear message and then probed for understanding. Instead, I proceeded, all the while keeping our timeline in mind and pressing for results. Sound familiar?

In order for meaning to transmit between you and your direct reports, you have to assume the onus for making sure they have decoded the message in the way you intended it to be decoded. The two ways to do that are to encourage questions in general and to ask specific questions in particular situations. For example, you might inquire, "Do you see any roadblocks to getting this done?" If I had done that in the training session, someone might have said, "Yeah, it doesn't make any sense." That would have been a valuable tidbit of information.

Send Nonjudgmental Messages

Using descriptive words is one of the best ways bosses can make sure that they are stressing observable, external, objective reality. These words focus the receiver's attention on the thing or action being described, rather than on the boss's personal reaction. Conversely, judgmental words show evaluation and stress personal reactions. They are words that direct the receiver's attention to the *emotion* rather than to the *description* of the event. This often engenders a defensive response in the receiver because judgmental words tend to be vague and abstract, and they annoy people.

"You" oriented speech, a particular kind of judgmental language, tends to focus on the receiver and often implies blame. Whether the evaluation is stated outright or merely implied, the receiver often reacts defensively. "I" language, on the other hand, shows ownership of reactions and reduces the likelihood that the hearer will react defensively. Notice the difference between these two:

> ***You misunderstood.***
>
> ***I haven't made myself clear.***

The former assigns the blame for the communication breakdown on the listener, while the latter indicates that the fault lies with the speaker. This may seem like a small thing, but over time, judgmental language feels like an attack, and its continued use stands in the way of building rapport.

One of the ways you can begin to use descriptive, concrete language is to begin sentences with "When…" and "The problem is…." Notice the difference in these two messages:

> ***You aren't showing much consideration to your co-workers.***
>
> ***The problem is, others have to assume your responsibilities***
> ***when you don't get here on time.***

The first lets the direct report know that there is a problem, but the defensive reaction will probably erase any willingness to find out more about how to be more considerate. In the second example, the person knows exactly what the problem is, and a solution is evident.

Another way to avoid defensive reactions is to try to use more unrestrictive language and fewer restrictive words. Restrictive words are words that attempt to control or restrict the actions of others. Consciously or unconsciously the sender's use of restrictive words implies that the receiver must express agreement. Using words like "should," "must," "always," and "never" can cause the listener to react defensively. Unrestrictive words offer a less rigid orientation because they suggest rather than demand conformity. Saying "maybe," "might," and "could," describe options without being aggressive. Also, using unrestrictive language shows more respect for the listener.

However, don't start to water down your message with unrestricted language when restricted messages are called for. "We might want to consider, if possible, following prescribed protocols to try to avoid negative patient outcomes, since people could possibly sue us into oblivion if we don't" is not the way to create a sense of urgency about a critical issue. Sometimes you have to use the stronger restrictive language, but don't overuse it, especially when unrestricted words will do the trick and avoid the problems that judgmental language creates.

Negative judgments usually cause the most problems, but even positive judgments are not without some caveat. I usually encourage bosses to give more positive feedback, but the words have to be genuine. Even if they are complimentary, if they are shallow or insincere compliments, they will trigger a similar defensive reaction to the negative judgments. Your message will backfire. Effusive, unwarranted praise is just as bad as none at all. The boss who is tempted to say something like, "This is the most brilliant expense report I have ever read. Have you ever considered joining Mensa?" will take huge strides away from effectiveness and nullify future attempts to give warranted praise.

Stick to the Facts

Like judgments, inferences are another source of problems in any communication situation, largely because the speaker treats the inferences like facts. Statements of fact are confined to what is observed and cannot be made about the future. Inferences go beyond what is observed and can concern the past, the present, or the future. Facts have a high probability of being accurate; inferences represent only some modest degree of probability. Most importantly, facts bring people together; inferences, like judgment, create distance and cause disagreements.

Facts bring people together; inferences, like judgment, create distance.

To illustrate this point, think of the last really heated argument you had with someone. Does this person share DNA, a last name, or both with you? How many statements of fact were actually articulated during this conflict? One? Two? Often these frenzied exchanges happen because our emotions overpower us, and we begin to communicate in inferences and judgments instead of facts. Even though we usually reserve our worst behavior for those whom we love most, sometimes we display it at work too. In either case, we let emotions interfere with us getting to the core of the issue by concentrating on the facts. Since facts tend to bring people together and further agreement, facts are usually rare in these kinds of exchanges, but they are critical to successful communication.

PROBLEM #2: YOU CANNOT <u>NOT</u> COMMUNICATE

Another source of communication breakdowns is incongruence between the words that people say and the nonverbal signals that they send, largely because we lose sight of the fundamental truth: You cannot not communicate. Every second that we are in the presence of another, we are constantly sending and receiving messages, often silent, nonverbal messages. These nonword symbols are the first things we notice about others and the first things they notice about us. They provide information about gender, age, preferences, emotions, and group membership.

One of the major problems associated with nonverbal communication is that it is not a precise language. There are no nonverbal dictionaries that provide the meanings for these symbols; nonverbals are often vague or unintended; nonverbal communication is continuous; and, compared to verbal communication, nonverbal communication is more highly prone to misinterpretation. Yet, studies show that over 60% of the meaning that is exchanged between the sender and receiver is related to nonword symbols. In other words, the very thing that people believe most readily is the least accurate. Is it any wonder communication problems are at the heart of so many disagreements?

Studies show that over 60% of the meaning exchanged between the sender and receiver is related to nonword symbols.

To further complicate matters, bosses often tell me that they didn't "intend" for people to take a message a certain way. The receivers have misunderstood. I can offer sympathy, but the reality is, our intentions don't speak as loudly as our actions. Unfortunately, like the road to another bad place, the road to high turnover is paved with good intentions.

For example, Dan was a client who was an extremely gifted and focused engineer. I didn't think there were any limits to his potential in his highly technical Fortune 500 Company. The only problem was, Dan had trouble connecting with people, and as a result, he experienced high turnover in his department. I had spoken to Dan over the phone and was very impressed with his verbal ability and responsiveness, so I couldn't imagine why he was having so much trouble. Then, I met Dan in person, and all questions were resolved. Dan wore a constant frown and look of discontent. Even when he was talking about something that he enjoyed, the frown persisted.

Rather than telling Dan about my observations, I decided to show him. I asked him to prepare a two-minute discussion that he might typically have

When there is a discrepancy, the receiver will trust the authenticity of nonverbal messages.

with a direct report. We videotaped the interaction with me playing his direct report. When I played it back, I turned down the volume and asked Dan to *hear* with his eyes. He watched himself scowl and glower for two full minutes. When I turned off the tape, I asked him to forget that he knew the nature of the discussion and to guess what the speaker had been doing. He said, "It looks as if I'm trying to explain quantum physics to an oyster," (a little engineering humor). Dan had no idea that his nonverbal demeanor was interfering with his effectiveness. In other words, his *intentions* had very little to do with the reality that he was alienating people with his facial expressions and glares. Once he understood what he was doing, he was able to correct the problem and retrain himself to look interested, not intimidating and scary.

Nonverbal communication is especially persuasive and powerful in communicating emotions. When there is a discrepancy between the words we say and the nonverbal message we display, the receiver, more often than not, will trust the authenticity of nonverbal displays of feelings more than the verbal explanation of them. Since these emotions are frequently difficult to control, they will often leak through in telltale hints about our nervousness, anger, boredom, or other feelings. However, we are not always aware that we are sending powerful messages that undermine the message we are trying to convey. To help understand some of the ways we sabotage our best efforts, here are some principles of nonverbal communication and their applications to the workplace:

Respect space. The use of space refers to personal space and territoriality. Personal space is the bubble that surrounds a person. Standing 18 inches or closer, in American culture, causes the other person to feel uncomfortable. Americans are most comfortable when others are at least an arm's length, three to four feet away. In many other cultures, standing that far away can result in the other feeling snubbed.

Territoriality refers to our "turf." At work, this would be an office, a desk, a computer, etc. We don't want others using our things, even though they are really the company's things. Before coming into our offices, we might want people to knock on the door frame, even when the door is open.

Violating personal space or territoriality will often trigger a defensive reaction.

Exude confidence. Action language includes motions, gestures, and posture. One of the things I coach executives about is carrying themselves in such a way that they communicate poise. *Looking* self-assured will cause others to believe that you are, even if you aren't. Standing or sitting tall with shoulders back communicates an air of authority. One tip I give clients is to avoid the temptation to put your hands in your lap when you are seated because doing so encourages the shoulders to slump forward. Tapping, nodding, and swaying are nervous habits that can detract from your professional image. Above all else, avoid pointing. This is the single most defense-building, intimidating gesture that a boss can use.

Shake hands with élan. The handshake, the first and probably most important, if not only, acceptable form of touch in the workplace, is extremely important because people assign so much weight to its merits. Men seem to know how to shake hands with one another, but often women don't practice shaking hands at all, and men don't know how to shake the hand of a woman. All the same rules apply. A handshake should be firm, not crushing. The entire hand should be involved, not just the fingertips; and both men and women need to avoid the temptation to turn the wrist of the other person, thereby putting your own hand on top of the other. This is usually seen as an act of aggression and is likely to start things on a negative note. With rare exceptions, other forms of touch in the workplace should be avoided. For the most part, neither sex appreciates the two-handed handshake or the handshake that involves touching the other's shoulder or arm.

Look them in the eye and mean it. Ironically, eye contact denotes both friendliness and aggression. Eye contact seems to occur when people seek feedback or reactions from others or when they want to signal that they want to communicate. It encourages interaction by signaling that the communication channels are open and that the receiver is ready to listen. In American culture, looking someone in the eye communicates honesty, warmth, and good will; lack of eye contact will often make people suspicious. People frequently interpret the absence of eye contact to be an indicator of disinterest, apathy, rudeness, or deceit. However, a gaze that lasts longer than ten seconds is usually seen as hostile or flirtatious.

Present a professional image. Physical presentation includes the objects we display that intentionally or unintentionally send messages about us. This, more than any other area of nonverbal communication, has received a great deal of attention. Books like John T. Molloy's *Dress For Success* gave us data upon which to base our decisions about professional dress and presentation. Nevertheless, trends like "business casual" cause us to revisit this area and to continue to question what we should be doing. Some general rules seem to pass the test of time, however. These are:

PROFESSIONAL PRESENTATION CHECKLIST

❑ Dress for the job you want, not the one you have. Buy expensive clothes, whenever possible, even if this means you will have fewer garments.

❑ Objects that identify you with a social, political, or religious group can alienate as many people as they attract.

❑ Gaudy jewelry, sunglasses, tinted glasses, and hair cream that makes the hair look shiny or sticky can detract from your professional image.

❑ Heavy scents, unruly hair, and unpolished shoes can be problems for both men and women.

❑ For men, hair that is off the collar and facial hair that doesn't exist or is neatly trimmed will send positive messages.

❑ For women, hair that is neatly styled, simple, and not too long or curly sends a positive message.

❑ For women, dark nail polish, long nails, heavy make-up, frilly or revealing clothing, open-toed shoes, spike heels, textured hose, and other trendy items may suggest that you are not serious business women.

For individual clients, this is the area that causes the most defensive reaction. People say that how they dress shouldn't matter. "My work and integrity should speak for themselves."

I agree, in principle, that these statements should be true, but they aren't. The truth is, others judge you on the whole picture, so even though it's your right to make whatever decisions you want with regard to your appearance, keep in mind that all choices have consequences, some good, others not so good. Do you really want to jeopardize your future for the sake of a haircut or clothing? Awareness of the impact that object language can have will equip you to make informed decisions about the messages you want to send.

Speak well. Paralanguage refers to *how* we speak, the nonverbal elements of the human voice. It includes all that accompanies language and consists of all the vocal cues that individuals use to communicate: pitch, rate, inflection, volume, quality, enunciation, flatness, and fullness. Awareness of paralanguage can help you show more interest and enthusiasm when words are presented in a more animated fashion. If your business calls for you to communicate via teleconferencing or phone calls, paralanguage will be extremely important for you since it will be the only form of nonverbal communication your receiver will have.

A problematic trend that has been sweeping the nation is "upspeak." This is an inflection in the voice that makes the speakers sound as though they are asking a question when they're actually making a statement. It's usually an attempt to elicit from the receiver some recognition of understanding. For example, a person might say, "So, I called Tim? The VP of operations? To see if they had fixed the supply chain problems? And he said he would call me back before ten." The questions seem to ask, "Do you understand?" "Are you following me?" But they also communicate uncertainty and a desire for approval. Both undermine the sender's position of strength. To improve paralanguage, tape-record yourself. Is your rate too fast? Voice loud enough? Statements declarative rather than questioning?

Create an environment for communicating. Environment refers to all the factors in the environment that influence the communication climate: temperature, seating arrangement, elevation differences, and color. Often appropriateness is culturally determined, but there are some general truths. People who are trying to communicate as equals should both have the same elevation. In other words, both should be seated or both standing. Barriers, like podiums and tables, between people create distance. King Arthur had the right idea about creating equality when he had the knights sit at a round table so that no one would be in any better position than anyone else.

Respect others' time. The use of time also varies from culture to culture. In America, being "on time" means participants are in place a few minutes early. Being "late" is anything after that. As I mentioned earlier, the boss who continuously shows up late to meetings with her direct reports sends a loud message that they are not important to her, no matter what her words might indicate to the contrary. People with status and power can show up late and get away with it in the short run; however, in the long run, not respecting the time of others can cost you in loss of trust and rapport.

Understand Culture

Another principle of nonverbal communication that further compromises effective communication taking place is that it is culturally learned and is dictated by cultural norms. Certainly, anytime we visit another country, we do well to learn their nonverbal language, even if we cannot master their verbal language. However, cultural norms exist within our borders too.

For instance, there are significant differences between the way men and women communicate via nonverbal communication. Women tend to smile more than men do, often when they are not happy. Research suggests this is a learned behavior that harkens back to the days when women were expected to be the peacemakers at home or at work. Since women often had subordinate positions in the workplace, keeping peace with the boss was a realistic and insightful goal. Although usually seen as a sign of positive characteristics like intelligence, good personality, and pleasantness, sometimes smiling is a demonstration of submissiveness. In fact, even chimpanzees smile when they wish to avoid confrontation with a higher status chimpanzee. The positions women have in organizations have been changing, but nonverbal communication often hasn't kept pace with other kinds of reality. It's a subtle language that today's women learned from their mothers, who learned it from their mothers, and so on back in history.

Similarly, women tend to nod when they are listening. Often another woman will decode this to mean that the listener is following the conversation, which is probably accurate. But most men will think she is agreeing with them since they usually don't nod unless they agree. Smiling and nodding are habits that most women have trouble breaking; therefore, when I coach a female nodder or smiler, I encourage her to make sure she is using clear, concrete language to communicate her real perceptions. This will help her mitigate the confusion caused by the nodding and smiling.

> *Smiling and nodding are habits that most women have trouble breaking.*

In the workplace, the purpose of communication is to enhance performance and produce better outcomes. But that isn't so easy. Particularly in difficult discussions, you will want to pay special attention to both the word and non-word symbols they choose. Flawed technique can quickly turn a meeting into a fruitless argument. In spite of your best efforts, however, you will sometimes find yourself either involved directly in a conflict or on the periphery of one, sometimes acting as a referee.

PROBLEM #3: CONFLICTS ARE TOUGH TO RESOLVE

Resolving conflict doesn't come easily to too many people. Most of us want harmonious relationships and smooth interpersonal interactions. However, we know intellectually that disagreements and conflicts are part of any dynamic organization. They arise because people care about their jobs and want to produce good results. Conflict is not always negative, however. Sometimes it should be encouraged when discussion and debate can generate creative, innovative approaches to issues or decisions. Conflict is beneficial when the focus is on finding the best solution. However, conflict is unproductive when it fails to produce mutually satisfying solutions or when it becomes personal in nature. When you are involved in a conflict yourself, consider these ideas:

❏ *Depersonalize the conflict*. Catch yourself when you begin to fall into the trap of believing that the other person is deliberately trying to make a situation difficult.

❏ *Clearly state your desire to find a solution* that will work for all involved before trying to resolve differences or conflict.

❏ *Build on areas of agreement* before you address areas of difference.

❏ *Listen first and talk second.* Ask open-ended questions to draw others out and to encourage them to talk about the conflict.

❏ *Try to arrive at a common goal around which everyone involved can focus,* and agree to work through areas of disagreement. In other words, don't agree to an outcome that you will not support. Articulate reservations that you have and talk with the other person until you can agree on a course of action.

❏ *Dig for understanding* without implying criticism.

❏ *Focus on common ground issues* and interests of both sides. Find a "win" for all affected parties and avoid entrenched positions.

❏ *Identify specific behaviors in concrete terms* and explain the tangible outcomes they have, so that the other person can more easily appreciate the nature of the difficulty.

❏ *Rely on facts* instead of judgments or inferences to help you avoid giving feedback that becomes personal.

❏ *Have a goal in mind,* a purpose for the meeting or discussion. Remember to put it in one sentence that attacks the problem, not the person. Secondary issues can divert or confuse matters. Ask yourself, "What is my goal in saying this?" Maintaining a helpful attitude will keep the other person comfortable and motivated to work with you to solve the problem.

❏ *Above all else,* before you give someone a piece of your mind, be sure you can get by with what you have left.

Sometimes the boss is not directly involved in the conflict. Instead, one or more of your direct reports are experiencing some problems. When this happens, the first rule is to stay out of it, if you can. Jumping in to fix things may work in the short term, but in the long term, you won't have created anything better. When one of the people

Usually, there should only be two people involved in the conflict.

involved approaches you and vents, the first thing you can try is to listen empathically. Then, when the direct report finishes explaining the situation, you can ask simply, "What would you like me to do with this information?" Usually the answer will be "Nothing." However, if it isn't, weigh carefully whether you should step in. Usually, there should only be two people involved in the conflict. Any more, and things get really ugly and complicated. Encourage the people to resolve things themselves.

However, sometimes you just can't stay out of a disagreement. When productivity starts to suffer or morale is compromised, something has to be done sooner rather than later. If both of the people involved agree that they can't work things out between themselves, the boss needs to get involved.

A beginning strategy is to have both people meet with you to discuss the plan for resolving their differences. But instead of hashing things out right then, invite the participants to fill out some pre-work. This will help you gather the information that will be essential to getting to the core of the trouble. One way to gather this information is to ask each person involved in the disagreement to answer questions before the actual meeting occurs. (See form in Appendix B, page 173.).

After the participants have answered these questions independently, they will be ready to meet with each other to discuss their answers. Let them try to do it alone to see if they can. If they can't, then have another meeting with you there.

This can be a slow, painstaking process, but it works. When each person is taking a turn reading answers to the other and then discussing the answers, volatile outbursts are unlikely. This technique requires time and patience, but it tends to be more successful than the "bandaid" approach. Eventually your direct reports will learn that friends may come and go, but enemies accumulate. Also, if they don't get the benefit of you taking their sides, they will soon tire of your objectivity and quit making a fuss about inconsequential things.

VISIBLE, VIRTUAL OR VERBAL:
SOLVE COMMUNICATION PROBLEMS

SUMMARY

Effective communication is at the heart of all human activity, so bosses who excel in it take great strides in developing their people and keeping the stars in the organization. However, visual, virtual or verbal, there are three problems that will compromise your ability to send and receive messages.

What are the roadblocks to effective communication?

1. Words don't mean; people mean.
2. You cannot not communicate.
3. Conflicts are tough to resolve.

Increasingly, an organization's competitive advantage depends on people, especially on creative, innovative people communicating effectively with each other and with you.

To maintain industry leadership of innovation, leaders can no longer rely on a few key individuals to develop creative solutions. Instead, bosses who want to attract, retain, and develop a pool of talented thinkers must know ways to encourage each person's contributions. Effective communication is one important way.

CHAPTER 4

COACH. YOU'LL PRODUCE HIGH SCORERS

*Criticism has the power to do good when there is something
that must be destroyed, dissolved or reduced, but it is capable
only of harm when there is something to be built.*
—CARL JUNG

Direct reports—people who need direction and leadership—rely on their leaders to give them feedback and mentoring, not just management and evaluations and certainly not scolding. However, the people who need help the most frequently lack the guidance that would move them to the next personal, team, and company success level.

Too often leaders are not prepared or trained to conduct an appraisal that stretches performance and ensures their direct reports' development. Instead, the appraisals become confrontational and judgmental; goals are not clear; neither person is prepared; and the discussion occurs when it's too late to do anything about the problem. Therefore, the performance appraisal is the most powerful and most misused tool for improving performance.

Picture this. A direct report comes in for a performance appraisal, and the conversation goes something like this: "Sue, thanks for coming in today. I've been wanting to bawl you out for about six months now, and today I have allotted an entire hour to really rake you over the coals. I'd like to start by pointing out all the things you have done wrong in the last year and let you know you won't be getting a raise. Specifically, I'd like to address the problems you're having with your ambiance, attitude, élan, esprit de corps, flair, and joie de vivre.

> The performance appraisal is the most powerful and misused tool for improving performance.

Then, in the last ten minutes of the hour, I want to talk to you about your goals for the upcoming year and say something really inspirational so that you will leave here all charged up to set the world on fire. How does that sound?"

As ridiculous as this scenario seems, the unfortunate truth is that many companies who conduct one performance management conversation a year are engaging in a version of this very thing. Occasionally you will encounter a misguided direct report who has the wisdom of youth and the energy of old age, but for the most part, people really do want to spend their time doing important work that is noticed and appreciated.

Today's employees and the organizations themselves demand direction from their leaders. Therefore, a well thought out performance appraisal system, clear expectations, reviews that inspire, and specific action plans are critical to the individual's and organization's success.

CREATE THE SYSTEM

The advantages of an effective performance appraisal system are many: better performance, improved relationships, coordination of personal goals and business objectives, identification of high-potential individuals, and justification for monetary rewards. However, much depends on the efforts that go into crafting the system.

The first step is to have clearly defined job descriptions that specify the tasks, functions, and responsibilities of each job. What does it take to do this job right? What are the success indicators? What are the derailers? Answers to these questions form the foundation for deciding behavior-based competencies for the particular job, the area of the organization, or the company as a whole.

Many organizations start by defining roles and responsibilities as they relate to the level the person holds in the organization: executive, manager, or employee. Other companies choose competencies that address certain areas of the organization, such as accounting, manufacturing, human resources, or sales. Once decision makers decide how to measure performance, they are ready to identify specific behaviors that demonstrate competency in relevant areas and to choose the scale that makes sense for them.

Usually competencies relate to one of four areas: ability to get results, capacity to form relationships, decision making, and leadership. Specifically defined competencies might also include business acumen, customer focus, coaching, integrity, vision, communication, teamwork, flexibility, technical skills, and innovation. Once the company decides on 8 to 10 competencies, the next step is to establish the rating scale.

The most basic scale is three points: exceeds expectations, meets expectations, or fails to meet expectations. However, a four-point scale gives more options for evaluation and forces the evaluator to avoid a middle-of-the-road review.

Once the decision makers have determined the criteria for evaluation, they are ready to set the timeline. In short, the year begins with goal setting, continues with ongoing feedback, and concludes with the end of the year evaluation that is often tied to raises and bonuses. This sort of schedule avoids surprises and the "once a year" mentality that doom most performance appraisal systems. Also, the periodic reviews give the employee a chance to take corrective action when there are still opportunities to make a difference.

> *The year begins with goal setting, continues with ongoing feedback, and concludes with the end of the year evaluation that is often tied to raises and bonuses.*

In general, four meetings per year work well. The first is a goal setting meeting; the second addresses progress on the goals; the third surfaces any problems that might interfere with the end of the year appraisal; and the final one is a formality that ties the progress to rewards. This does not imply that ongoing feedback should not take place between meetings. On the contrary, the four-meeting format is the minimum number of meetings you should have with your direct report. Even though bosses often resist adding more formal meetings per year, they soon learn that the increase in productivity and morale among their direct reports more than compensates for the extra time they commit to the process.

CLARIFY EXPECTATIONS

The simplest way to raise satisfaction and meet objectives is to lower expectations. However, most organizations have a more global perspective: they want to make money. Lowering expectations doesn't make that happen. If your direct reports were honest about the goals they had committed to during the previous year, the goal would have been something like, "I will bounce from one artificial and contrived emergency to another like a badly hit ping-pong ball." Of course, no one plans to spend time doing that, but judging from the vast numbers of individuals who achieve that goal each year, you have to wonder what exactly they initially set out to do.

The purpose of goal setting with your direct reports is to tie their individual performance to the organization's mission, vision, and values and to link short-term objectives to long-term targets. As the boss, your first challenge is to understand the organization's direction so you can help your direct reports figure out how they will play a role in meeting the organization's goals.

Retired Air Force Colonel Dick Anderegg stated that, based on his knowledge of and tenure with the military, failure to tie vision to individual efforts is the single biggest mistake he has seen new leaders make. As Col. Anderegg pointed out, when people didn't know *exactly* what the mission was, they let the organization "wander into tasks that the organization didn't have the skills, training, or resources to complete successfully. It's hard to have 'vision' when you don't know which way to look." Whether leading a military unit or a part of an organization, your direct reports rely on you to set the direction and to keep them from wandering. As the boss, you need constantly to be posting a mental "You Are Here" sign for your direct reports, not asking "You are where?"

> *As the boss, you need constantly to be posting a mental "You Are Here" sign for your direct reports, not asking "You are where?"*

If history teaches us anything, it should be the importance of clearly defining objectives so that we don't accidentally create a fiasco. The Bay of Pigs Invasion, the Tet Offensive during the Vietnam War, and the Challenger tragedy are a few examples of the devastation that occurs when people allow unclear goals, hidden agendas, or conflicting agendas to distract them from their objectives. As the boss, part of your job is to make sure you don't let your direct reports digress from the direction the organization needs for them to take.

We know that people are most committed to goals they've helped construct. Therefore, when you and your direct reports work together to clarify these goals, they will be more likely to *commit* to rather than *comply* with the efforts that will drive success. Well-written goals serve a variety of purposes: they create opportunities for objective, fair dialogue; they define the "score card" that will be used to determine rewards; they energize and motivate; and, most importantly, they focus efforts.

As the boss, your job is to help them keep that focus. Think of yourself as an optometrist, and your direct report as your patient. As you discuss goals, ask, "Better now, or now? Better now, or now?" By constantly tweaking the focus, you will take great strides in assuring that you and they are looking through the same lens. But how do you do that when you already have too much on your plate? In short, you help them work smarter, which, in the long run, will reap benefits.

By now, almost everyone has learned about SMART goals, objectives that are specific, measurable, attainable, relevant, and timely. *Specific* and *measurable* mean the goal is concrete, clear, and descriptive to the point that results can be measured. For instance, giving feedback that a direct report "needs to be more positive and have a better attitude" is not helpful. Identifying the particular improved behaviors is: greeting others, smiling, saying "thank you," and giving praise.

"Attainable" might have already been a source of disagreement between you and your direct report. Your perception of results that are achievable and realistic might differ from those of your direct report. When this happens, here are some questions for you to consider:

- ❑ What are others in this role accomplishing?
- ❑ What is this person's history of goal attainment?
- ❑ Does this person have the experience, knowledge and capability to do this?
- ❑ What evidence is there to come to this conclusion?
- ❑ Are you and your direct reports so far apart in your perceptions that you feel as though you're in different time zones?

The *relevant* aspect of the goal is also critical, but both bosses and direct reports continue to make some fundamental errors in this area. First, all goals are not created equal; they need to be prioritized. People are often motivated to work on things they like, things that are familiar, or things that are easy. That's why we spend inordinately more time checking e-mails than we do making difficult phone calls. We'll check e-mail *all day* before we'll make a tough call. But frequently these initiatives are not the most critical. You need to be sure that the *timely* elements of effectiveness are considered: first things are done first, deadlines are met, and direct reports separate important from unimportant uses of their time.

Second, the people involved fail to define the parameters in which the goals will occur, so the boss has one set of expectations and the employee another. If a condition of goal attainment is "with no overtime" or "with our current equipment," these limiting conditions need to be spelled out so no one is surprised. If there are disagreements about these conditions or if the direct report considers the conditions unrealistic, the goal setting meeting, not the end of the year review, is the time to surface those issues.

Surprises are best left for birthday parties, not performance reviews. One way to do this during the goal setting meeting is for you to ask,

Surprises are best left for birthday parties, not performance reviews.

"What factors might interfere with your achieving this goal?" This question alone can help to put things on the table and resolve differences in the early stages of planning. If a direct report answers, "Well, the fact that the software is from 1988 might cause some setbacks," you need to be ready to step in to correct these roadblocks.

A third problem is direct reports often don't understand their parameters for accountability and decision making. They either overstep when boundaries are not clear—for example, you just found out that your team just opened a new factory in China that you knew nothing about—or they err on the side of caution and risk-avoidance and never leave their cubicles except to go to the bathroom.

Working together, you and your direct reports can clarify which decisions they will make alone, which ones will require them to notify you, and which ones they need to clear with you. When the direct report is either not making decisions or is running to you with every problem, both parties are wasting time and efforts, and you are overlooking chances to develop talents and potential among your direct reports.

Another problem is direct reports tend to be too cautious in setting their goals; therefore, you will need to challenge them to stretch. But to do this, you must constantly communicate your willingness to let them fail once in a while. A person who doesn't fail occasionally probably isn't playing in a tough enough league. Of course, you will monitor their progress and make sure the failure isn't too devastating to them or the organization, but you won't want to be too cautious either. Confucius had a great point of view for bosses to espouse: "Our greatest glory is not in never failing but in rising every time we fall."

Finally, bosses frequently do not support the efforts of their direct reports. The research suggests, and multi-rater feedback reports confirm, that mentoring, giving feedback, and developing others are usually the boss's lowest ratings, primarily because "getting the job done" is more important. But if you ignore your direct reports too much, the job may "get done," but your team will also be "done" and move out the door.

Diane's story is a typical illustration of this phenomenon. Diane, a director in a midsized Midwestern consulting firm and top performer, confided during a coaching session that she had no idea how her boss, the Chief Operation Officer, perceived her performance. She observed, "I wouldn't be surprised to get a $10,000 raise next year, and I wouldn't be surprised if I got fired." Because her boss was consumed with COO duties related to "getting the job done," he neglected his role as coach and mentor. Two years after Diane made this observation to me, she left. Although independent and resourceful, Diane needed to know what was expected of her, how she would be evaluated, and where she could go for the help to improve. She couldn't get answers to any of her questions, so she took her talent to a competitor.

A fact that Diane's boss and others overlook is that developing others is "the job," a significant and critical part of the job. Coaching others is only one part of a boss's job, so taking care of other responsibilities often takes precedence. Many organizations reward solo performance and individual efforts more than they recognize coaching others. For an appraisal system to succeed, companies need to recognize and reward efforts related to leading and managing others. That may not happen in your part of the world, at least for now. But, it's something that you can begin to change quickly—perhaps even before you finish reading this chapter.

Your support is an inexpensive but effective way to improve performance and show your commitment to excellence.

Whatever system your organization adopts, your support is an inexpensive but effective way to improve performance and show your commitment to excellence. Frequently managers don't have the authority to give financial rewards, but all bosses can give the intangible rewards of attention, coaching and mentoring. Furthermore, through discussion, you can learn what other kinds of intangible rewards your direct reports might appreciate—increased responsibility, more interesting work, variety, opportunities to work alone or on a team, etc. The key is to build trust that the boss cares and wants to respond to the needs of the direct report.

REVIEW PERFORMANCE GLADLY

Another way to build trust and reduce anxiety is through scheduled conversations. Obviously, feedback about performance should occur when it can do the most good—when it is immediate and focused.

When a direct report makes a mistake, addressing the problem right away is the surest way to take corrective action. Similarly, when a person excels at a task, complimenting and praising the efforts immediately will show appreciation and encourage more of the same. Certainly, giving specific, timely feedback to direct reports concerning both their successes and mistakes is critical to helping them develop. However, having more formal review sessions is also important to the direct report's development. Regularly scheduled reviews avoid the end of the year angst and allow employees to receive feedback when there is still time to take corrective action.

One of the reasons these critical discussions are not occurring is bosses feel uncomfortable, unprepared, or ineffective in such encounters. They usually have no problem when they can heap praise, but when there's been a problem, it's another story. They're not sure how to begin: "Uh, John, can we talk about the order for 10,000 parts that you shipped to Iceland that were supposed to go to Islip?"

Even though these kinds of discussion are not easy, bosses tend to avoid the very conversations that could help them build better relationships and increase productivity among the people who need their direction and support. One way for you to improve your coaching is to follow the GLAD Communication Method, the step-by-step approach that was introduced in Chapter Two. This method can also help you improve performance appraisals and inspire peak performance:

G et to the core of the performance issues.

L isten to the other first.

A dd your own ideas.

D evelop an action plan.

Get to the Core of the Issues

Although you may have several issues to discuss with a direct report during a performance review, getting to the core of the performance issue means focusing the discussion on actions or behaviors, related to one thing at a time, one thing the person can control and change. Sometimes this will mean having several discussions within the same performance review. Dividing is conquering. When you introduce each issue separately, you and the direct report can avoid the problems associated with lumping things together. Instead of talking about eating an elephant, you concentrate on what it will take to eat two bites of it in the next 30 days. People may not like any part of eating the elephant, but thinking about two bites will be easier than thinking about eating the entire thing.

> *People need to hear the things they are doing well so that they can leverage their strengths, but they also need to identify improvement areas.*

When bosses discuss a direct report's performance problems with me, it does seem they are trying to deal with an elephant. So, the first question I ask is, "When is the last time this person did an outstanding job?" If they ever did, it was usually two jobs ago. Hard work, dedication, and integrity will help a person advance quickly in many industries, but sooner or later, critical thinking or its absence start to influence a person's ability to get the job done.

If decision-making or problem-solving capacities are interfering with the person's performance, the problem may be an *inability*, rather than an *unwillingness*, to do the job. In that case, you need to consider alternatives to either give direct reports additional help or to move them to an area that is better suited for their abilities.

In general, the performance review should be focused on goals, balanced in nature, and candid. People need to hear the things they are doing well so that they can leverage their strengths, but they also need to identify improvement areas. Ordinarily going through each of the goals that was set at the beginning of the year is unnecessary. More often, one or two goals will be a more obvious concern. Starting the conversation by identifying those will help to keep the discussion on track and build momentum for addressing them.

Listen to the Other First

The second step in the GLAD system is to listen to the other first—to elicit that person's ideas and opinions before offering your own. Starting on a positive note can be helpful in this step. For instance, after identifying the issue, the boss can say, "Brag on yourself a little. What have you been able to do about _____?" This will do two things. It will help direct reports know you are listening, and it will give you a chance to understand more information. (But you've really got to listen. If you're taking phone calls and checking e-mails, what are direct reports thinking? They're wondering, "I wonder if my resumé is up to date.") This step also gives direct reports a chance to make sure accomplishments are not overlooked or forgotten, and it's your chance to check on the accuracy of the review.

The performance appraisal should be a two-way conversation, an opportunity for both the boss and the employee to learn.

The performance appraisal should be a two-way conversation, an opportunity for both the boss and the employee to learn. Listening to the other person first shows a willingness to consider new information, and if necessary, to change the nature of the review. Similarly, *hearing* the other person sets the tone for the give-and-take that will be necessary to create understanding and commitment between the two. Asking your direct reports what information they would like to receive from you and then telling them what you would like to hear from them can further open the communication channels between the boss and the direct reports.

Before moving to the next step of the review, take advantage of the opportunity to address as many issues as possible with open questions. Asking the employees to talk about their perceptions of problem areas will reduce the defensive reaction that result from you giving a solution. When bosses jump in to fix things, some direct reports get so defensive that you'd think it's football season and they've hired their own defensive coach. But you can avoid that kind of reaction. For example, you can ask, "What things do you still need to do to improve?" or "What are some ideas for correcting that problem?" As mentioned in Chapter Two, "What?" and "How?" are the magic words that open the discussion.

One way to develop your open questions is to ask yourself, "If this person were doing this perfectly, what would I see?" This will help you brainstorm a list that defines excellence. For example, in working with a regional manager of a large grocery store chain, I asked him to imagine what a perfect store manager would be doing. He came up with these:

❑ She's walking around talking to customers.

❑ She's there for part of every shift at least once a week.

❑ She keeps track of her paperwork and complies with company policies.

❑ She makes sure payroll is adjusted when sales are down.

> *Tell people what to do, and you'll end up working inordinate amounts of time because you will be doing their work and yours.*

Each of these bullets can then become an open question during the discussion. "Sue, how might you improve your customer orientation by being more involved with them?" She might push back that she's already doing all she can, but you can always focus on doing more for the sake of improving. Tying this to a benefit will sweeten the deal: "Sue, I'd like to recommend you for a raise this year, but I can't do that until your customer satisfaction scores improve, so what are some things you can start doing to improve those scores?" The essence of the questions is what can they start doing, stop doing, or do differently? Once you put these concerns in question form, you will be ready to listen to their ideas and help them develop them more completely. Think of this step as a game of *Jeopardy*. If it's in the form of a question, you're still in the game. If it's a statement, the buzzer goes off, and you get no points.

Another part of this step is paraphrasing what the other has said—summarize ideas and reflect emotions. Often a summary statement is more powerful when followed by another open question. For instance, the boss can restate the message by saying, "So you're not worried because you think this will work if you give it enough time. *How* will you address the deadlines that are in place already?" A series of these kinds of statements and questions can frequently lead the direct reports to conclusions they had not previously considered. The trick is to concentrate on responding nondefensively when people express viewpoints that are contrary to your own.

Are you thinking, "This will take so long! I don't have time to ask a lot of questions. It's so much faster to just tell people the problem and tell them how to fix it"? During performance reviews and routine conversations, *telling* people what to do will always be the most economical use of time, at least in the short run. However, you are likely to create a bunch of lazy people who rely on you for all the answers, who don't make decisions because they know you will, who avoid taking on more responsibility, and who are glad for the buck to stop with you, not them. These people will become the monster direct reports. You will work inordinate amounts of time because you will be doing your work and theirs, and instead of a win-win situation, you end up with a whine-whine state of affairs.

Add your own ideas

In a perfect performance appraisal, the discussion should have implied a course of action for the direct report, but most of you don't work in a perfect world. Even if you have done your best to focus on one topic and to understand the position of the direct report, the review won't be going in the right direction. You will need to paraphrase more and ask more How?/What? questions to guide the discussion. If you've done all that, and the conversation still isn't going where it needs to go, the third step is the time for you to tell your direct reports your views of the situation.

Clearly defining the specific behaviors that the direct report should address will help to keep the discussion focused. Give *concrete* feedback that lets the direct report know *exactly* what you're talking about. If you disagree with the employee's assessment of the situation, if there has been a shift in priorities, or if you two disagree on action steps, this is the time for you to express ideas and concerns and discuss how to resolve differences. The direct report needs a clear understanding of what you expect and what to do more of or less of to improve.

Remember to communicate the "why" behind the "what." However, communicate clearly that *results* matter. Be careful not to confuse their well-intended activities with results. Many corporate improvement efforts have negligible impact because they have little to do with the company's goals. An activity-centered program confuses ends with means, process with outcomes. It assumes that activities related to performance improvement will automatically ensure that profits will improve.

A results-driven approach bypasses the lengthy preparations for success discussions to concentrate on specific, measurable performance indicators. Direct reports convey that they appreciate this level of candor when there's still time to take corrective action. For example, if you were to say, "I would like to recommend the same bonus that you received last year. However, based on ____, I wouldn't be able to do that if this were your end-of-year evaluation," this would be an eye-opening message that would resonate with the direct report and streamline the year end evaluation.

(D)evelop the Action Plan

Many companies discuss compensations, raises, and bonuses in one end-of-the-year discussion—the same discussion that addresses goal setting, feedback, evaluation, and action planning. When all this is lumped together in one meeting, the meeting that happens is a type of postmortem. Even though it's too late to do anything that will make a difference, direct reports are somehow supposed to be motivated to charge into the upcoming year, more focused and productive. It doesn't work that way. On the contrary, they are angry and resentful, especially if they have had no warning that their performance was substandard.

The first phase of action planning should take place at the beginning of the year. The action plan is a fluid document, however, that should change with new information, accomplishments, unexpected events, and learning. At the beginning of the year, and at each subsequent meeting, you and your direct reports need to prioritize goals and objectives to identify the current most important two. Even though the direct reports might write several goals at the beginning of the year, ongoing discussions between you and them should reexamine the importance and relevance of each objective, the current two most important "what's" and "how's" they will address in the next 30, 60, 90 and 180 days.

Keep in mind that timelines help this process. When you tell a direct report, "I'd like to have a status report on this in two weeks. How is the 15th at 10 o'clock for you?" you'll be more likely to see a sense of urgency on the part of the direct report. Of course, new initiatives or demands can alter plans, but by scheduling follow-up conversations, you will take steps to ensure results. The main payoff of the action plan is not the form or the document but the discussion. Once you and the direct report know what is needed and expected, each of you has identified roadblocks, and the timeline is clear, the action plan apparent, and the results more likely.

There seems to be something magic about writing the action plan. It is the tangible agreement between you and your direct report. It is a way to track results and redirect efforts. It is also something that you can pull out during the next conversation and refer to. If direct reports have accomplished the objective, you'll be able to check off that task, which will communicate your knowledge that it was done. If they haven't achieved the results you both agreed to, the words on the page will serve as a glaring reminder that you haven't forgotten their commitments. Therefore, both the boss and the direct report should keep a copy of the original agreement and the subsequent notes and changes. When this happens, the end-of-the-year evaluation brings no surprises.

ACTION PLAN FOR OBJECTIVES	
Objective *What* I Will Do	*How* I Will Accomplish This
1st Objective:	30 Day Goal: 60 Day Goal: 90 Day Goal: 180 Day Goal:
2nd Objective:	30 Day Goal: 60 Day Goal: 90 Day Goal: 180 Day Goal:

COACH, YOU'LL PRODUCE HIGH SCORERS

SUMMARY

Most performance appraisals and performance management systems are not what they could be, primarily because the system is flawed, and the participants are not prepared. However, creating a coaching culture, one that is characterized by clear goals, ongoing mentoring, scheduled reviews, and focused action plans, is likely to create a more productive culture.

What do direct reports need so they can achieve better results?

1. An effective, companywide system.
2. Clear goals and objectives.
3. GLAD performance reviews.

When they have all three of these, employees can more often achieve their potential and contribute to organizational goals.

Much depends on you. Understanding how your behavior shapes the behavior of your direct reports is the first step. Once you realize that you can and should influence performance, you need to learn and practice the skills associated with performance management. Even though this all takes time and effort, the rewards are impressive and immediate. After all, you want people to follow you for reasons other than mere curiosity. Good performance reviews will give them that incentive.

CHAPTER 5

MAKE PEOPLE GLAD TO GET RESULTS

The future is not the result of choices among alternative paths
offered in the present—it is a place that is created—
created first in the mind and will; created next in the activity.
—WALT DISNEY

A firm but fair F² boss knows that being good to your people is one part of the equation; keeping your eye on the results is the other part of it. Whatever your organization, even in the nonprofit sector, your company exists for a reason, and part of that reason is tied to results and staying financially solvent. As simple as that may seem, however, today's bosses have a more complicated arena in which to play the games of organizational solvency. That game requires new and better ideas for attaining the results that your company expects. Great advances have always come from ideas, but ideas don't fall from the sky; they come from people. People write the software; people design the new products; people start new businesses. Every new product or service is the result of human ingenuity and creativity. Yet, bosses often don't know how to help their direct reports engage in more creative problem solving so that they can hit the target every time.

Moving ideas to action is the fundamental responsibility of every boss. First, there must be great ideas; then there must be stellar performance.

> First, there must be great ideas; then there must be stellar performance.

The two must exist in tandem. Certainly action without good decisions is no better than superb ideas with no action; but repeatedly people are uncertain about what they need to do to turn ideas into action, an uncertainty that can drain motivation from the best of employees. Bosses need ideas to make sure they don't play a role in depleting the resources of their best and brightest so that they seem as lifeless as mannequins. Bosses that no one wants to leave understand that wherever creative problem solving, sound decision making, and accountability go, innovation, motivation, and economic growth are sure to follow.

ENCOURAGE CREATIVITY

Creativity is not a tangible asset like equipment or facilities. Rather, it can be inferred from a company's expansion and success. It is the ability to produce novel and useful ideas. Creativity and competitiveness in the global market place go hand in hand, and both are good insurance policies for organizations that want to attract and retain talent. However, encouraging creativity in direct reports is the second step. Discovering it in yourself is the first.

> *Encouraging creativity in direct reports is the second step. Discovering it in yourself is the first.*

Bosses who tend to rely too much on their own problem solving abilities would do well to learn from history. During World War II, the statistician Abraham Wald taught a lesson about what happens when people either don't have the capacity to look at all angles of the problem or who don't utilize the insights they have. Wald was called upon to assess the vulnerability of airplanes to enemy fire. The data showed that some parts of the planes were hit disproportionately more often than other parts. Military decision makers who were asked to evaluate the data concluded that these parts should be reinforced.

Wald, however, had a different conclusion. He explained that the parts hit least often should be protected. His recommendation reflected his insight that the decision makers were only considering planes that returned. Wald reasoned that a plane would be less likely to return if it were hit in a critical area, and that a plane that did return, even when it had been hit, had probably not been hit in a critical location. Therefore, he argued, reinforcing those parts of the returned aircraft that sustained many hits would be unlikely to have the desired results.

Wald's lessons for bosses are numerous. First, you must be certain that you have all available data. That means analyzing both successes and failures of internal and external initiatives. The obvious answer isn't always the right one, and often your direct reports will see this. Discipline yourself to listen to them first, before you disclose your theories or solutions. If they know what you think, they will either echo your ideas or develop intellectual laziness. Why should they bother thinking about solutions if you have all the answers? Next, you need to look for creative problem solving within yourself and among your direct reports.

How do people learn to be more creative? According to researchers at the University of California, one of the best answers is tied to understanding the components of creativity: expertise, creative thinking, and task motivation. Expertise is the foundation of all creative work. The potential for creativity is enhanced when your direct reports have abilities, knowledge, proficiency, and expertise in their fields of endeavor.

Expertise is the foundation of all creative work. The second element of creativity is creative thinking skills, the analytical capacity to see the familiar in a different light.

In other words, when people understand their jobs thoroughly, they are better able to know how to experiment with new and innovative approaches to conventional methods. Providing opportunities for them to augment and hone this expertise can pay huge dividends both immediately and ultimately.

The second element of creativity is creative thinking skills, the analytical capacity to see the familiar in a different light. Personality traits, such as intelligence, independence, self-confidence, risk-taking, a tolerance for ambiguity, and perseverance in the face of frustration are strong indicators of creativity. Unfortunately, these traits are difficult to develop. Therefore, when creativity is needed, hiring people who have already demonstrated these traits can prevent future frustration for you.

Finally, task motivation turns creativity potential into actual creative ideas, which eventually turns into innovative initiatives. This desire to work on something because it's interesting, exciting, satisfying, or challenging seems to determine the extent to which individuals will fully engage their expertise and creative skills. Creative people often love their work, but establishing a work environment that is conducive to inspired problem solving can also affect motivation to carry out the creativity. Work environment stimulants that foster creativity include a culture that

- ❑ encourages the flow of ideas
- ❑ makes fair evaluations of ideas
- ❑ rewards creative work
- ❑ provides sufficient resources to support ideas

As the boss, you can play an important role in encouraging creativity by communicating openly, showing confidence, and encouraging trust among members of your group.

Another thing you can do is to enhance your own creativity. How do you do this? The simple answer is by doing something different, something that is outside your regular routine and comfort area. When I began working with Stan, he was a dynamite boss whose direct report respected and liked him. By all objective and subjective measures, Stan was doing a great job. That's why his company invested in his development. The decision makers at his company recognized that Stan was high potential, and they felt certain he would one day run the company. Many would say, "It wasn't broke, why did you mess with it?"

The reason they had come to that conclusion was Stan had potential to be more than he was, the promise to be a superior, not just above average leader. The one thing standing in the way of his greatness, however, was his own lack of creative problem solving. Certainly, Stan was a great analytical thinker, always at the ready to get to the core of the problem and formulate well thought out solutions. But even these skills wouldn't be enough to ensure his continued success at the helm of a technology company, the kind of company that would need creativity to stay on the cutting edge.

A mind stretched to new dimensions can never retain its original shape.

By interviewing Stan, I learned that he reads avidly: *The Wall Street Journal, Forbes, Time*, at least two daily papers, and several industry journals. Stan was already doing the first thing I encourage clients to do—read at least an hour a day. I asked him about the last time he read fiction or poetry. He grimaced. He said he had not read anything like that since leaving college, and *Beowulf* had left a bad impression of fiction. I asked him about the last time he saw live theater. This time he winced. This was stuff he didn't like. His idea of entertainment for an evening was seeing a sporting event, not that there's anything wrong with that.

I then quoted Stan one of my favorite axioms: "A mind stretched to new dimensions can never retain its original shape." Stan was doing a great job of exercising the parts of the brain that were already working, but he wasn't doing such a great job of stimulating and stretching the creative part of the brain. To help him begin this process, I asked if he could commit to reading one novel and seeing one play before we met again. He agreed, reluctantly, but added that his wife would probably send me flowers for suggesting they see a play.

When people haven't read fiction in quite a while, I often recommend something on the best-seller list, something that they can talk about with others who are also reading. In most of 2005, that was *The Da Vinci Code*.

If you hadn't read this novel, which dominated the number one and two spots on *The New York Times* for months, at cocktail parties they would make you sit in the non-*Code* section.

But I met Stan before the *Code*, so I recommended anything by Pat Conroy, my personal favorite. I usually encourage clients to start with *The Lords of Discipline* or *The Great Santini* since most people enjoy page turners that are also sassy and well-crafted, both hallmarks of Conroy's writing. Often clients report that they enjoy Tom Clancy and Michael Creighton, too. Start experimenting until you find someone you like and then find other authors who are similar. Once you have a positive experience with fiction, I encourage you to explore other writers and to commit to reading at least one novel a month.

Stan did read a Conroy novel and even went to see a Shakespearean play with his wife. He said he enjoyed both and committed to continuing to explore this side of himself. In addition to stimulating his creative thinking, Stan had discovered a new and different way to enjoy his leisure time. I doubt he'll give up golf and watching sports, but I never had that in mind in the first place. I just wanted him to explore some yet unexplored territory.

The next thing Stan and I talked about was his need for ongoing support. We worked together for 90 days, but I wanted him to have encouragement as he advanced through each level. Ideally, there is someone in the organization who can give some of this—a boss, mentor outside the department, etc. But more often, this kind of mentoring needs to come from outside the organization, especially if you are the CEO.

Stan and I began to explore options for him to set up a mastermind group, a group of people who meet regularly to discuss their problems and to seek the counsel of the others. Mastermind groups exist in all kinds of professions and have made huge differences in the advancement of their participants. In Stan's case, I challenged him to come up with the names of three people who understand his business and industry but who don't compete with him. Since Stan is in technology, he needed to find people outside his company who had faced similar issues and challenges. He wasn't able to think of five initially, but he did identify two others.

> Mastermind groups exist in all kinds of professions and have made huge differences in the advancement of their participants.

The next step was for Stan to contact them to see if they would be interested in participating in this kind of group and to explain to them how it would work. Ideally, all the participants will live in the same geographical location so they can meet face to face, but that isn't always possible. Sometimes, scheduled conference calls have to substitute.

Usually the participants agree to the length of the meetings and then divide the time equally. For instance, if there are three participants, they might choose to meet for 90 minutes, with each person allocated 30 minutes. People can use their 30 minutes in whatever way makes sense to them that month. Of course, confidentiality is expected, and sometimes participants even ask the other members to sign confidentiality agreements. Typically, the group tries to meet once a month, but often scheduling conflicts prevent that, so the participants agree to meet quarterly. Each group develops its own rules of engagement, such as a member who postpones a meeting will assume responsibility for rescheduling with the others.

Peer-to-peer coaching can work at all levels of an organization, but I have found it to be most beneficial at the upper echelons where peers are scarce.

Another alternative to the mastermind group is peer-to-peer coaching. This can work at all levels of an organization, but I have found it to be most beneficial at the upper echelons where peers are scarce. The owner of a convenience store chain found this to be true, so he teamed up with another owner in a different geographical location. They have exactly the same kinds of problems, but they never compete for the same customers. Therefore, they are able to give each other insightful advice and guidance without the worry of disclosing any secrets. They have a call scheduled once a month that allows each man 30 minutes to talk about whatever is on his mind.

The main principle related to increasing your capacity for creative thinking is to avoid the idea that you have to go it alone. Use resources that you have, friends, coaches, board members, and even your direct reports to help you analyze issues from a variety of perspectives. Think out loud. Many people don't know what they know until they talk about it, so find a good sounding board and articulate possibilities. Stop yourself if you hear the words, "I have always..." or "I usually...." Ask yourself if the current problem is really identical to ones that you have solved in the past. If they aren't, and they probably aren't, start exploring new solutions. If you find yourself uncomfortable with a suggestion or proposition, ask yourself why. Another technique is to force yourself to assume far-fetched ideas are correct and that your position is wrong. In other words, force yourself to look through a different lens. Once you start thinking in these terms, you will be better equipped to help your direct reports stimulate their own resourcefulness.

The most underused but most effective technique for inspiring creative problem solving is brainstorming. Yet, instead of engaging in true brainstorming, most teams jump in to start evaluating. Or, the boss speaks first, which essentially shuts down any original thinking because direct reports already know what the boss thinks and wants. So, you shouldn't speak at all, or you should speak last in a brainstorming session. Here are some other steps to improve imaginative thoughts:

- ❑ Write down a clear statement of the problem you are trying to resolve. Put it in one sentence that begins, "The problem is...."

- ❑ Develop a set of criteria that you will use for evaluating solutions. Don't evaluate yet, just generate the criteria. For example, name obvious constraints like "Using our present facilities" or "without losing market share."

- ❑ Describe what the ideal solution would look like. Identify three or four "success indicators."

- ❑ Generate a long list of ideas or solutions. Don't evaluate. Work as quickly as someone can capture the alternatives on a flip chart. Since the nonsensical idea of one person might trigger a brilliant idea in someone else, there are no stupid ideas in a true brainstorming session.

- ❑ When the ideas stop coming, it's time to move on. Only now will the group be ready to evaluate the ideas. Can ideas be combined? Old processes reworked?

- ❑ Assess the alternatives against the criteria previously identified.

- ❑ Examine the pros and cons of each idea from the perspective of each stakeholder group.

- ❑ Continue to explore alternatives so that the group can choose the best solution or solutions.

MAKE THE TOUGH DECISIONS

Even though the process can be time consuming and often tedious, avoid the temptation to run with the first idea or solution that seems to work. Instead, push back and challenge the group to dig deeper, explore more fully, look further. Continued creative problem solving generates inspired decision making. Working together, encourage the group to identify key factors in a complex problem, associating seemingly unrelated information in order to analyze and simplify the critical concerns:

- ❑ Champion calculated risks.
- ❑ Stimulate discussion of possible consequences.
- ❑ Separate important from unimportant topics. Talk about how to concentrate efforts on the few key factors that will move ideas forward.
- ❑ Integrate the big picture with the details of making the solution work, and develop a plan for implementation.
- ❑ If possible, test the plan with a small group of people and get their feedback before rolling out a large-scale initiative.

MOVE IDEAS TO ACTIONS

What helps to motivate people? Unfortunately, for many companies, their methods are wrong.

Their motivation technique of choice is to frighten employees until they are immobilized, and then reward everybody with a worthless gift that bears the company logo. In turn, the employees learn to spend an inordinate number of hours of "face time" at work being burnt out and practically useless. Ideas don't become actions with this kind of approach.

However, there are techniques that do help. In the past decades, anecdotal evidence has suggested that the boss can have an active, positive effect on moving ideas to action. These findings revealed that what bosses expect of their direct reports and the way they treat them help to determine performance outcomes. In other words, superior bosses who communicate high performance expectations often have direct reports who fulfill them.

For example, in 1961 Alfred Oberlander, a manager at Metropolitan Life Insurance Company, noticed that new agents performed better in outstanding agencies than in average or poor ones, regardless of their sales aptitude. Therefore, he decided to group his superior agents in one unit to provide a challenging environment. The performance over the first twelve weeks far surpassed expectations, showing that when the problems created by poor producers are eliminated, the efforts of the focused and determined can have more impact. In short, Oberlander's conclusion was that if you set high but realistic expectations, the stars will rise because they try to live up to the image the boss has of them and do what they know stars are expected to do.

A couple of years later Oberlander noted that the performance of superior agents who had been grouped together continued to rise to meet their manger's expectations, but the performance of the weaker ones, who had been left in underperforming units, declined and attrition among them increased. In your world, if the stars shine more and the weak ones eventually eliminate themselves, how will your overall productivity change? My guess is you will end up better off because you will be able to give your attention to the people who will drive success instead of being distracted by the ones who will probably never produce anyway. Are you motivating your strong people or creating a situation in which they are motivated? What difference does it make as long as the outcome is the same?

> If you set high but realistic expectations, the stars will rise because they try to live up to the image the boss has of them.

In *Good to Great*, Jim Collins talked about getting the right people on the bus in the right seats to drive the bus in the right direction. In order to accomplish this, Collins advocated hiring people who are already motivated to do the job well. Hiring the best, brightest, most highly motivated people is the single smartest things a boss can do because when you do, you don't have to worry too much about motivating them. They come factory equipped with motivation. I also agree with theorists who say bosses can't motivate people. But you can sure *demotivate* them.

As motivational theorist Frederick Herzberg put it, "I can charge a person's battery, and then recharge it, and recharge it again. But it is only when one has a generator of one's own that we can talk about motivation. One then needs no outside stimulation. One wants to do it."

Similarly, Herzberg noted that the boss can give a direct report a kick in the pants, a physical or psychological KITA, but this approach has three major drawbacks:

1. It is inelegant.
2. It contradicts the precious image of benevolence that most organizations cherish and is at odds with F^2 Leadership.
3. Since it is an attack, it directly stimulates the autonomic nervous system, and the direct report just may kick you back.

Above all else, the KITA does not lead to motivation, only movement.

The avoidance of the things that demotivate people isn't the same as motivation. People expect a competitive salary, good working conditions, security, status, and good interpersonal relationships from their place of work. Other "perks" of yesteryear are now also expected: 401K plans, medical insurance, paid vacation, paid holidays, and, in some industries, tuition reimbursement. If a company doesn't offer these, people won't seek long-term employment there. But these things don't motivate employees; they just keep them from leaving.

The most efficient way to sabotage any empowerment or motivation program is to have meetings with your people during which you punish them for decisions they made while, at the same time, encouraging them to think for themselves. Eventually, these direct reports will become numb, the feeling they will experience right before hopelessness, an emotion that is often suffered right before shutdown or departure.

People are motivated by achievement, the feelings they get from a job well done, recognition for achievements, the work itself, responsibility, and opportunities for growth or advancement. Studies show that when these conditions prevail, people indicated a marked increase in their liking of their jobs, lower absenteeism, and a much higher rate of promotion.

What, then, should a boss do to make sure that he or she is not demotivating direct reports? Create a system that inspires motivation. As Stephen Covey pointed out, "So often the problem is in the system, not in the people. If you put good people in bad systems, you get bad results." Sounds as if he's echoing the conclusions Oberlander reached at Metropolitan Life, doesn't it? In addition to making sure your best people are working with other stars, here are some steps you can take to help their people stay focused, engaged, and motivated:

❑ Communicate, set time frames, establish goals, and get out of the way. Talk to others about *what* needs to be done, but let them decide *how* they will go about it. Unless their way is wrong, let them experiment with their own methods. In other words, be crystal clear on *what, when,* and more open to *how.*

❑ Direct reports will not be motivated to reach high levels of productivity unless they consider your expectations realistic and achievable. When the goals aren't realistic, people become disheartened. Stretch them; don't snap them. Dangling the carrot just beyond the donkey's reach will just make for a very angry donkey.

❑ Help people formulate personal goals that are consistent with organizational and department priorities. Take care of your people, and they will take care of their jobs.

❑ Working with others, break large projects into several smaller steps with deadlines for each step. Track completion and give balanced feedback on the success of the plan.

❑ Give each person whole projects instead of pieces or parts of a project.

❑ Grant authority and freedom to get the job done. Let them sign their names, making them personally responsible for the quality and accuracy of their work.

❑ Assign specialized tasks that enable people to become experts.

❑ Remove controls, but retain accountability.

❑ On a regular basis, introduce new and more difficult tasks not previously handled.

As this list implies, accountability is at the heart of motivation. We are motivated to put our best efforts into projects that are our "babies." To continue the metaphor, when we babysit someone else's baby, we only worry about managing safety until the parents return. We don't worry about equipping the child for the future, piano lessons, education, braces, moral development, or the host of other things parents think and worry about. Instead, we try to bide the time and make it as pleasant as possible.

Unfortunately, some people don't see their work as their own because they don't feel responsible for outcomes, largely because the boss is in the middle of things, often micromanaging. Dan was one such boss. He routinely worked a seventy-hour week. I asked him to walk me through his day. How many e-mails did he read? Voice mails? Meetings?

> *Some people don't feel responsibility for outcomes because the boss is in the middle of things, often micromanaging.*

We discovered that in an average day, Dan read about 100 e-mails and listened to about 20 voice mails. He had six direct reports that he was micromanaging. We did the math. If each of these six direct reports wanted to talk to him "for just a minute," which was actually never less than 10 minutes, he was averaging about an hour a day in "for just a minute" conversations. He was averaging about an hour and a half a day reading e-mails that he had been copied on; and he was spending another 40 minutes listening to voice mails that said, "I just wanted to let you know...."

On a daily basis Dan was spending over three hours doing things that he shouldn't have been doing, things that were not ultimately in the best interest of his direct reports or the company. I asked Dan if there were anything at all he'd rather be doing with 20 hours a week than spending them at work. He answered with a nonverbal, "duh." I then asked Dan if he would like to learn ways to routinely change his 70-hour workweek to a 50 hour week. He seemed game, if not more than a little suspicious.

I pointed out to Dan that bad accountability was at the heart of most of his problems. His direct reports weren't sure what decisions they should be making alone, which ones should involve him, and which ones should involve someone else. Actually, they were pretty sure that all decisions should involve Dan, and they were right. He felt very insecure about letting out the reins with them. Dan needed to learn ways to remove the controls while retaining accountability; he needed to increase the accountability of each person for his own work.

I encouraged Dan to begin the process by asking each of his direct reports to list the major decisions he or she was making. Then, using the assigned code, to indicate what level of involvement the direct report thought appropriate: making the decision alone, notifying Dan but proceeding without further authorization, or consulting with Dan before going forward. Then, I suggested that Dan meet with each of his direct reports individually to discuss whether they agreed about the level of accountability of each decision.

> You need to start a leadership pipeline that is continuously fueled by new people.

I assured Dan that he could retain as much control as he thought appropriate but that he would be encouraging the development of his people if he not only allowed them to make their own decisions but also insisted on it. I also explained that he needed to start a leadership pipeline that was fueled by new people all the time. As Dan was relinquishing power to his direct reports, he needed to be talking to his own boss about taking on new, more challenging work himself. Notice, this does not mean more work; this means more challenging work that is appropriate for new levels of responsibility within the company.

Dan tried my suggestion and was amazed at the immediate and profound payoff. People were doing their own work; they weren't coming to him with problems they should be solving; and he was leaving the office at a decent time each day, the first time that had happened in five years. Dan also noticed that he was growing in his own development since he now had time to devote to learning about his next level of responsibility. And his golf game got better.

On the next page is the accountability chart that I encourage my clients to use. This is a fluid document that should change periodically. In fact, many bosses think it's helpful to put timelines on each decision. Other bosses have found that putting parameters around certain decisions is helpful too. For instance, working together you and your direct report may decide that up to a certain dollar amount the direct report will make the call; at another level he or she will notify you; at another, consult with you before moving ahead. Over time you should start to notice that the direct report is making good decisions at one level of difficulty or complexity and that the person is ready for more rein.

ACCOUNTABILITY CHART

Directions: Identify the major decisions that you make on a somewhat routine basis. Then, using the letters at the top, identify the level of accountability that you think is appropriate, not what you are currently doing. If you are responsible for the outcome but don't have the authority to make the decision alone, put an R under your name and the corresponding letter under your boss's name or the other person who needs to be involved.

A = Authority to make decisions alone
R = Responsibility for completing the task
N = Notification—Boss or other person is notified of decision
C = Consultation—Boss or other person must OK before proceeding

Major Decision/ Task	Direct Report	Boss	Other's Name	Other's Name

Even though this process takes time initially, usually about an hour of your time with each direct report, the reward is the 20 hours a week that Dan started to get back. The process intimidated Dan initially, but after several weeks of using it, he reported that he couldn't believe the difference. He still had his finger on the pulse of things but wasn't troubled with the day-to-day responsibilities of each of his direct reports.

Here are some of the objections that my clients raise when I suggest this. "If my boss comes to me for an answer, I won't have it at my fingertips." That's true. You might have to start saying, "Karen is taking care of that. I'll call her and get right back to you." It's an illusion to think you are in control of the truly important stuff anyway. If people want to mess things up, they will. Fortunately, most people don't set out each day to make a mess of themselves at their jobs. You can spend 70, 80, or 100 hours a week at work, and no matter what you do, you won't prevent every problem. So why not spend a reasonable number of hours at work, have some free time to recharge, and accomplish more in the long run?

> *Adjusting* their *behavior won't be as tough as adjusting your own.*

Another argument I hear is, "They will still come to me for every little thing." They will if you let them. You have made them dependent on you, so they won't want to be responsible for things that you were always willing to take the hit for. When they call, e-mail, or drop by for "just a minute," ask them where that issue is on their accountability chart. Then tell them you have complete faith in their ability to handle things, and they should come back only if they are stuck or don't know what to do. If they come to you for an answer, don't give one. Ask them what they think one or two ideas for solving the problem are, and then tell them to go do the right thing.

Trust me. Adjusting *their* behavior won't be as tough as adjusting your own. They are probably hungry to feel more connected to their work, more responsible for their own outcomes. In general, decisions should be made at the lowest possible level, but with that comes the authority to carry them out. You can't jump in and fix things if there is a glitch. You can coach them through it, but if you are there to clean up after them, what is their motivation to do it right?

MAKE PEOPLE GLAD TO GET RESULTS

SUMMARY

*Want to achieve more impressive results
and lead a motivated work force?*

Forget gimmicks like "casual day" dress codes. Unless your primary objective is to lower the status of your direct reports by cleverly appearing to give them a benefit, allowing people to dress in bad clothing one day a week won't be motivating.

While you're at it, forget punishment, forget shallow compliments, and forget unrealistic raises. These things won't work, but you can still make them GLAD to get results:

1. Hire motivated people and make jobs as interesting as possible. Then and only then will you be able to quit worrying about employee motivation.

2. Encourage creative problem solving at all levels of the organization.

3. Make the tough decisions.

4. Move ideas to action.

If you have people in jobs, use them. If you aren't using them to their fullest potential, if you are overlooking opportunities to discover creative solutions, if you aren't letting them be accountable for their own work, something isn't right. Either you have the wrong person, or you are duplicating work. If you micromanage by breathing down the necks of your people, you might as well do their work yourself and save the company some dollars.

On the other hand, if you find ways to enrich work by creating responsibility, growth, learning, and advancement, you will not only make them GLAD to get results; you'll take yet another step toward becoming the magnetic boss that no one wants to leave.

CHAPTER 6

NEVER RUN OUT OF ALTITUDE, AIRSPEED & IDEAS AT THE SAME TIME

Among those whom I like or admire, I can find no common denominator, but among those whom I love, I can: All of them make me laugh.
—W. H. AUDEN

A sense of control over our destinies is one of the most basic of human needs. When we feel in control of a situation, we feel empowered and focused. When we don't, we get discouraged, and in the worst-case scenario, we start to feel like victims or aggressors.

Since most people spend the majority of their waking hours at work, it stands to reason that they look for many of their psychological needs to be met there. If these needs for control aren't realized at work, people soon become frustrated and unhappy, a surefire recipe for departure. Bosses can't control many things at work. In fact, they probably can't control most things, but they can control their own *reactions* to unfortunate events. Only then are they able to help their direct reports feel authority over their reactions to unpleasant and unexpected changes.

> Since most people spend the majority of their waking hours at work, they look for many of their psychological needs to be met there.

When hard times rear their ugly heads, bosses have to be the heroes, the rescuers who look after others and help them keep from losing their perspective and their coping resources. Like accomplished, safe pilots, bosses need to maintain altitude, airspeed, and ideas.

In his work, *Mysterium Coniunctionis* (The Mysterious, Mystical Union), psychologist Carl Jung explained the path of the hero and offered some insights about how the true hero faces and overcomes adversity:

> In myths the hero is the one who conquers the dragon, not the one who is devoured by it. And yet both have to deal with the same dragon. Also, he is no hero who never met the dragon, or who, if he saw it, declared afterwards that

he saw nothing. Equally, only one who has risked the fight with the dragon and is not overcome by it wins the hoard, the "treasure hard to attain." He alone has a genuine claim to self-confidence, for he has faced the dark ground of his self and thereby has gained himself... He has arrived at an inner certainty which makes him capable of self-reliance, and attained what the alchemists called the *unio mentalis* (the unity of mind).

Notice some of the lessons Jung has for you. First, there is no heroism in not ever having adversity to conquer. On the contrary, we admire most those who have fought the fight and won, not the ones who have never had a fight to fight. Second, Jung pointed out that the same dragon will devour some people and will be conquered by others. The dragon, or the adversity, remains the same; but the person opposing the dragon is different. When you

> *Even if you are a change agent who loves variety, you may realize that you only like change over which you have control.*

develop the necessary coping skills to fight adversity, you maximize the opportunities for emerging victorious, and you can then help others fend off the dragons too.

Workplace dragons usually involve change—unexpected, unwanted, and unwelcome change to the world as we know it. Even if you are a change agent who loves variety, champions innovation, and becomes annoyed with too much predictability, you may realize that you only like change over which you have control. When you face an unwelcome change, you may have as difficult a time adjusting as the change averse do. When you face this kind of dragon, you will need to hone the coping skills you already have and learn new ways to help you adjust, coping skills that bosses don't usually use enough.

Becoming aware of the value of augmenting coping behaviors can increase our understanding of the powerful role they can play in helping us bounce back from the hardships that change and adversity often bring. In other words, these skills can give us a modicum of control in situations when we would otherwise feel as though we had no power over our destiny.

THE VIETNAM POWS

Why do some people conquer the dragon, and others are devoured by it? I wanted to know the answer in order to understand why some bosses can win the hoard and enjoy the treasures that are hard to attain while others are not able to do either. I decided to study heroes, people who had overcome some sort of huge adversity and emerged healthy and hardy. I wanted to draw from their experiences in order to advise leaders about ways they can help themselves and others weather the storms that inevitably affect organizations.

To find these answers and to better understand how resilient people handle adversity, in 1995 I moved to Pensacola, Florida, to study the repatriated Vietnam Prisoners of War at the Robert E. Mitchell POW Center. The lessons I learned were surprising, almost shocking.

In 1973, 566 Vietnam POWs were repatriated to the United States. Evidence from prior captivity situations indicated that there had been high incidences of Post-Traumatic Stress Disorder (PTSD). Fifty to eighty-two percent of the WWII POWs who participated in the studies, particularly those who were imprisoned in the Pacific theatre, received a diagnosis of PTSD. Forty-seven to ninety percent of the Korean POWs in the studies received a similar diagnosis. Because of these staggering numbers, in 1976 the Navy began to study 138 repatriated Vietnam POWs. In 1996 they reached surprising conclusions about the data they had been collecting. In their 20-year follow-up, the researchers found that only about 4% of the Vietnam prisoners of war had received a diagnosis of PTSD. The researchers had expected better results; we had no idea that they would be so good.

The Vietnam POWs who were imprisoned, tortured, isolated, and beaten, had no higher incidence of PTSD than the average people in the average American city.

The data are astonishing when comparing the Vietnam group to the other captivity situations, but they are also shocking in light of the implications of these numbers. To give a frame of reference for understanding this, at any given time in a metropolitan area, about 1 to 4% of the population is experiencing symptoms of PTSD because of violent crime, natural disasters, or other kinds of trauma. In other words, this group of people, who was imprisoned, tortured, isolated, and beaten, had no higher incidence of PTSD than the average people in the average city in America. How can that be? I went into this study wanting to study communication and the links between communication and resilience. I had no idea I would stumble upon such astonishing results and impressive data about resilience.

The study participants told me that there were four main forces in the POWs' lives that helped them remain resilient: a belief in God, patriotism, a dedication to each other, and a sense of humor. These men personified the importance of never losing altitude, airspeed, and ideas at the same time. Even though their captivity indicated they had obviously run out of all three at the same time in a

> *Great bosses are people who can stay resilient in difficult times and help their direct reports do the same.*

literal sense, in a metaphorical or psychological sense, they were able to sustain all three. Great bosses are people who don't run out of them either; they are people who can stay resilient in difficult times and help their direct reports do the same.

ALTITUDE—MAINTAIN A GLOBAL PERSPECTIVE

Psychologists tell us that human beings want power and authority over their futures. We want to feel that we have a say in how things will go for us. When we perceive that our actions will make an outcome likely, we feel optimistic and secure. When we don't, we feel insecure. We feel like victims. Sometimes people stay in a victim's frame of mind after a loss or disappointment. They doubt their capacity to make their lives happen according to their own aspirations, so they wait to be rescued or blessed by good fortune. They start to feel undermined and overwhelmed, and they can become totally immobilized.

But the VPOWs weren't victims. They were certainly *victimized* by their captors, but they never saw themselves as victims, no matter what was done to them. They weren't victims because they took *control* of the few things they could control. They were told when and what and if they could eat; they were told if and when they could shower, sleep, and use the toilet. They had no say about parts of their lives that people normally take for granted. But they did have control over a few things: their humor perspective, their commitment to one another, and their involvement in a well-defined structure, all ways that allowed them to keep their "altitude."

In a physical sense, altitude is the elevation of an object above a certain level, usually the earth. Therefore, "altitude" as it applies to leadership, is a global perspective, a realization that there is a bigger picture and no one person is the center of the universe. When bosses indicate that they have altitude, they usually exhibit these behaviors:

❑ Vision—an ability to see the future and to anticipate consequences.

❑ Critical thinking—the capability to go into uncharted territory. Managers have the ability to do the right thing well; leaders have the ability to figure out what the right thing is.

❑ Prioritizing—the ability to do first things first and to separate important from unimportant uses of time.

❑ Motivation to look beyond the obvious.

❑ Skills to paint credible pictures of possibilities.

❑ Eagerness to create competitive strategies.

Admiral James Stockdale was one of the senior leaders of the POWs who embodied the characteristics and behaviors that indicate "altitude." He had the Code of Conduct to rely on to help him keep his global perspective, but no prisoners had experienced what these men were suffering. Therefore, he was challenged with the daunting task of making new decisions about torture, ones that no training or education had equipped him to make. He issued orders for the POWs to resist giving information and signing propaganda statements but not to risk permanent physical or psychological harm. When he issued this order, he feared he'd be court marshaled upon his return to America. Instead, because of his global perspective and "altitude," he will be remembered in military chronicles as a hero who was responsible for saving the lives of many and ensuring the resilience of hundreds of others.

"Leadership" does not always emanate from the leader, however. One of the stories that lives in the POW histories and clearly illustrates the importance of keeping altitude involved a lieutenant who had been shot down in an F-4 Phantom. The captors tortured him to reveal the maximum airspeed of the F-4. He told them the top speed of the F-4 was 500 knots, a number that is much lower than the actual maximum speed. The captors said they knew he was lying because a major had just told them the speed was closer to Mach 2. Thinking quickly, and trying to avoid torture for himself and the major, he retorted, "Well, that guy is a major. I'm only a lieutenant. They don't let lieutenants fly as fast as they let majors fly."

By keeping his wits about him, this young lieutenant was able to anticipate the consequences of his answer and to venture into uncharted territory, something that training had not prepared him for. He was certainly trying to take care of himself and his fellow POW, but he wasn't trying to be funny. However, stories of his quick wit soon spread throughout the POW community and validated their awareness that through humor, they could claim some control over what was happening. Aviators understand altitude in a real and a metaphorical sense, and you can learn to too.

There were many reasons the VPOWs fared better than those of other captivity situations: they were older, all volunteers, better educated, and trained in survival techniques.

There were many reasons the VPOWs fared better than those of other captivity situations: they were older, all volunteers, better educated, and trained in survival techniques. But the fact that they were almost all aviators is key too. Before they went into captivity, these aviators joined a system that encouraged cohesion and not only tolerated humor but often encouraged and revered it.

Humor of this stripe is sometimes called gallows humor—bleak, ridiculing, mocking humor, a different class of humor, perhaps, than many of the people we know would use. But it works for people who need to have a sense of control over death, and it can work for those of us who face less devastating kinds of hardships. During times of adversity, there is much we can't control, but our global perspective, our altitude, is one thing we can take charge of. Sometimes humor helps with that, and looking out for each other almost always does. Not losing airspeed is another thing that helps.

AIRSPEED—DEVELOP RELATIONSHIPS

When we think of airspeed, we think of velocity and the forces that make us go forward. Countless studies indicate that getting the job done is only part of the boss's job; building relationships to keep the right people doing the job is the other part of it. Relationships are one of the main sources of fuel that helps successful bosses accelerate their productivity and that of others. The boss who avoids running out of airspeed tends to have these traits:

- ❑ A knack for building relationships.
- ❑ A strong motivation to follow through.
- ❑ A willingness and availability to listen.
- ❑ A genuine interest in people.
- ❑ The capacity to convey respect for people and their ideas.
- ❑ The confidence to tell people what they need to know, not just what they want to hear.

Communication is the primary tool that helps us form relationships and develop closeness in our personal and professional lives. For the VPOWs, however, communication was difficult and sometimes nearly impossible; yet, it became a priority from the time one of the early POWs realized he wasn't alone.

In 1965 Bob Shumaker, one of the first POWs, had gone 133 days without face-to-face contact with another American. I want you to imagine what that must have been like—133 days without conversation, interaction, or communication. For over four months, Bob Shumaker endured solitary confinement, but he knew there was another American in the complex because he had seen him through the cracks in his walls. All the POWs emptied their waste buckets in the same latrine area, so Shumaker was able to observe Hayden Lockhart each day as he went about his routine. Realizing the POWs were going to need a plan and a communication system, Shumaker was determined to make contact with Lockhart. But he wasn't sure how he wanted to do this. Finally, he decided that he would write a note on toilet paper and leave it for Lockhart.

Shumaker decided to write a three word note on a scrap of toilet paper and hide it behind a piece of cement in the latrine they both used. He wanted to be very careful about what he wrote on this piece of toilet paper—it couldn't be very many words, so it had to be exactly the words he needed. So, on this scrap of toilet paper Bob Shumaker wrote three words, three words that in essence said, "scratch your area where your mother *specifically* told you not to scratch in public." His thinking was two-fold. First, he wanted to write something that Lockhart would know only another American would write so that he wouldn't suspect the guards were trying to trick him. Second, he wanted to devise a signal that would not arouse suspicion if the captors saw Lockhart doing it.

He wrote the note on the scrap of toilet paper, and day after day, he stood peeking through the cracks in the mortar in his room, and day after day, Hayden Lockhart came out of the latrine and made no signal. *Finally*, one day, Hayden Lockhart came out and made a huge display of scratching the region in question and facing every part of the compound. Years later, retired Admiral Shumaker told me that the most complicated communication system in history was born with a scratch of a crotch. It was a fitting and funny preview of how the POWs would use their communication system to bolster the spirits and morale of each other through humor. Even though they had created a way of communicating, they realized its limitations and knew that they needed other methods.

Several months later Bob Shumaker was assigned some roommates that he could talk to directly, but the guards forbade communication among the cells, a prohibition that the VPOWs disregarded. When the men had visual contact they used a version of the mute alphabet to signal messages to each other. Sometimes, when they were fairly certain they wouldn't be heard, they spoke through the walls. But these methods were limited.

Even though they knew they were restricted in the kinds of communication they could use, they realized the necessity of uncovering every possible option. One of Bob Shumaker's new roommates, Smitty Harris, remembered the "tap code" that he had learned during survival training. Because the POWs could tap almost all of the time, the Tap Code became the most sophisticated communication system they had. It is a 25-letter alphabet that forms a table of rows and columns, with the "C" and "K" used interchangeably. The letter "F," for example, is the second row first column and would be two quick taps to indicate the second row and then one tap to indicate the first letter of the row.

A	B	C	D	E
F	G	H	I	J
L	M	N	O	P
Q	R	S	T	U
V	W	X	Y	Z

It was an arduous task to tap a message one letter at a time, but the POWs quickly became proficient at the code and spent hours each day committed to staying in touch with each other. Originally, this was devised to be a system for getting policy throughout the POW camp, but it quickly became a way for staying connected to one another, keeping morale up, and for sharing jokes.

To give you an idea of what this tap code meant to the POWs for helping them maintain their connection with one another, their airspeed, VPOW Jerry Coffee wrote:

> I was beginning to decipher far more than letters and words from my unseen comrade. From subtle variations in his tapping, I could feel urgency, longing, sadness, excitement, and humor. I could tell if he liked my joke, or if it had bombed, depending on his extemporaneous scratching, drumming with the fingernails, brushing, or light thumping. What was he doing? Laughing or groaning? I was really beginning to know. It also became a source for feedback. "All that I learned about tapping those few days would become the heart of an incredibly effective system facilitating our mutual support and survival. To help each of us return with honor. By applying the communication system persistently and creatively, we would breach the barriers of brick and concrete and vast spaces in between.

The last line encapsulates what humor and communication do for all of us: They help us *breach the barriers of brick, concrete, and vast spaces in between*. These men risked dire consequences to communicate and share humor. The torturous "rope trick" was the punishment they suffered if they were caught. This cruelty dislocated the shoulders and created such pain that any man who experienced it gave the captors whatever information they demanded. It broke every single person upon whom it was used, 100% of them.

Admiral Stockdale, who is often remembered for being the vice-presidential running candidate with Ross Perot, endured torture more than most of the POWs because he was one of the senior ranking officers. The captors knew there was a communication system, so they tortured

Stockdale to give up the system and the players in it. They tortured him one day almost to his breaking point, with the promise that if he did not tell them what they wanted to know the next day, they would torture him again. Knowing that he was close to capitulating, Stockdale returned to his cell that night, broke a window, took a shard of glass, and cut his wrists. He had been willing to die to protect the communication system. The next morning, the captors found him in a pool of his own blood, unconscious, and they never tortured him again. Stockdale knew he was protecting something vital when he attempted to end his life for the sake of a communication system that the POWs would need to stay resilient and hardy.

> *Stockdale knew he was protecting something vital when he attempted to end his life to protect a communication system that the POWs would need to stay resilient and hardy.*

Stockdale's perception that the communication system was vital to their survival is borne out in countless illustrations of the POWs using communication and humor to help them through tough times. For example, after being tortured, Tim returned to his cell in terrible shape, needing the care of his roommates. Tim, who had attended Annapolis, was grateful for the concern his fellow prisoners were showing him but uncomfortable with all the attention. One roommate approached him and asked gently, "Tim, how you doing?" Tim shook his head in disbelief and said, "You know, guys, this place gets any worse, and it's gonna be worse than my first year at Annapolis."

Even though he was enduring his own pain, Tim took the opportunity to make his roommates laugh, and he hoped, to ameliorate their discomfort at seeing him in such bad shape.

Relationships, communication, closeness, and humor, all are fuel for us, airspeed that keeps us going through adversity and helps us help others. A global perspective equips us to realize that we aren't the center of the universe and that our problems pale in comparison to those of some others. Communicating with those that we care about or who rely on us allows us to keep this perspective.

Altitude and airspeed are two critical elements for any boss's success, but there's one more: ideas.

IDEAS—REMAIN FLEXIBLE

Creative problem solving is probably one of the most essential talents a leader can possess. Bosses who can look at diverse information and see relationships, who can reason abstractly and make logical connections, and who can think of the future as open and malleable bring an invaluable asset to their organizations: ideas. When leaders have ideas, they can solve unfamiliar problems and make decisions that are in the best interest of their direct reports and the organization, skills that are tied to the following:

❑ An openness to brainstorming and creativity.

❑ The motivation and enthusiasm to challenge existing processes.

❑ A knack for inviting input from a variety of perspectives.

❑ A willingness to experiment with novel approaches and champion innovation.

The POWs found themselves in a drastically altered world, one that they had never encountered before and, in spite of some training, one for which they were ill prepared. But like great leaders throughout history, they had the ability to engage in creative problem solving. They had ideas. They understood that the bend in the road wasn't the end of the road because they had the agility to turn, often repeatedly.

One of the classic stories of the POWs that illustrates this agility and willingness to experiment with novel approaches involved Jerry Venanzi and his motorcycle, a story that quickly became a legend in the POW community. One day, Jerry Venanzi was walking around outside his cell, a rare privilege, when he noticed some of the other POWs were staked out and being treated miserably. Seemingly there was nothing he could do to help them, except he thought he might have an idea for making them laugh and showing his camaraderie.

To distract the POWs from their discomfort, Venanzi put on a show for them. He created an imaginary motorcycle, which he pretended to get on and ride around the compound. His fellow POWs started to laugh, perhaps in disbelief. Being somewhat of a ham, Venanzi realized that this idea was indeed funny, so he staged a spill, feigned an injury, and limped. In an apparent plea for sympathy (and laughs), he hobbled over and showed them his burn or displayed some other kind of motorcycle injury. His act was so convincing that some of the POWs later tapped to one another, "Has Venanzi lost it?"

One of the things that the POWs found most humorous, however, was that the commander of the compound was caught up in Venanzi's ruse. He finally called Venanzi in and told him that he had to get rid of the motorcycle. As the commander pointed out, it wasn't fair. All the POWs couldn't have motorcycles, so Jerry Venanzi shouldn't be allowed to have one either. Venanzi reluctantly got rid of his imaginary motorcycle. (The exact dispensation method of the bike is not clear, however).

However, since he was disappointed about the loss of the motorcycle and since he was in solitary confinement, Jerry Venanzi decided to compensate for his disappointments by creating an imaginary companion, a monkey that he named Barney Google. The stories of Barney Google flew like wildfire through the POW community. They were not only grist for the POW mill; they let the POWs know that they could be heard through the voice of Barney.

Jerry Venanzi took his imaginary monkey to interrogations, confrontational meetings with the captors, and when Venanzi was asked questions, he would suddenly turn to the imaginary monkey and say "NO! I'm not going to tell them that! Because, if I tell them that, they'll beat the hell outta me! You're just going to have to shut up." The interrogator then asked, "What did he say?" (Who was in control during this interrogation?) Venanzi seized these opportunities to protest, "He's sick of the food. It's lousy food and he's tired of it. We don't have enough blankets, we're freezing to death." Whatever their grievance was, Barney voiced it on behalf of the POWs.

During one interrogation, the camp commander offered Barney tea, an offer Venanzi declined on behalf of the monkey, since Barney didn't like tea. This subterfuge continued for quite some time, all the while fueling the POWs' feelings of having some degree of control, if only to their reactions and their openness to finding ways to stay connected to one another through these kinds of shared experiences.

Finally, one day, the captors once again called him in and said that he would have to get rid of the dirty animal because Venanzi would be getting some roommates. The captors were certain the roommates wouldn't like the monkey. Of course Venanzi disagreed, but he finally capitulated and let Barney go on to another life outside the walls of the Hanoi Hilton.

I have told this story many times, but in 1999 I had the opportunity to present my research at a convention in Washington, D.C. to clinical psychologists. Colonel Venanzi lived in the D.C. area at the time, so I invited him to attend the speech. As usual, I went through this story and then said, "I have never had the honor, after telling that story, of introducing Jerry Venanzi." I then introduced him. The audience members had all kinds of questions for him and, generally, he reported that he thought that I had done a good job of representing what had happened. But then he reminded me that he had answered a letter I had written to inquire about the accuracy of my written account. I read his response to the group:

> Dear Linda,
> What you have written hits home and is generally factual, as I remember it. However, one point does stand out, and I do hope you can correct it before it goes finally into the history books. Barney is a chimpanzee, not a monkey. In fact, he used to get very upset when he was called a monkey. I do hope this can be corrected, (for Barney's sake of course).

The letter brought some laughs from the psychologists who were eager to ask Jerry Venanzi more questions. He didn't miss a chance to continue the joking. They asked him what his remembrance was of Barney. He said, "Well, Linda forgot to tell you something, but she may not have known this. Barney used to cheat at cards, and I couldn't trust him." He obviously loved looking around the room at the raised eyebrows of the psychologists who wondered about my claims that mental illness was not widespread in this population. Jerry Venanzi is a man who *still* has ideas about how to make people laugh.

Ideas are certainly critical for leaders, but leadership is not only about position, experience, knowledge, and education. It's also about the willingness to experiment with possibilities to help solve problems that no one has encountered before. Certainly Jerry Venanzi was a man who assumed this leadership function through his use of ideas. Doug Hegdahl was another, but he was barely a man.

Doug Hegdahl was a 19-year old seaman who, in violation of policy, went out on the deck of a ship during a thunderstorm and was washed overboard. A Viet Cong fishing boat picked him up and took him to the Hanoi Hilton. However, he wasn't like the other prisoners there. He was the only nonaviator, and he was only a teenager. He quickly realized that he could trick the captors into thinking he was dimwitted or simple because he couldn't have answered any of the questions they asked him about aviation, even if he had wanted to. He did not know about flying; he did not have intelligence about targets; he did not know the answers to any of their questions. Since his captors were confused about this very different kind of prisoner, Hegdahl had an idea.

To create more confusion for the guards, he started sucking the pen they gave him and leaked ink all over himself. When the captors asked him to write a propaganda statement, he asked them how to spell a word, such as "American." Hegdahl's ruse had immediate and enormous implications. The captors underestimated him and made the tactical error of putting him in a cell of one of the POW leaders, Dick Stratton.

Dick Stratton is the person who is best remembered as the POW who was on the front of *LIFE Magazine* doing the "Manchurian Candidate" bow that caused speculation in the United States about the POWs being brainwashed. Clearly a man of ideas himself, Stratton was the perfect mentor for the young Hegdahl. Under the tutelage of Dick Stratton, Doug Hegdahl memorized the names of over 200 fellow POWs, a significant feat that took important steps toward guaranteeing their safe return. (If a POW is known to be alive, according to the Geneva Convention, the captors have to produce that POW at the end of the war. To do otherwise would have invited international criticism for the Vietnamese).

Dick Stratton groomed Doug Hegdahl, and Stockdale, the acting senior leader, ordered Hegdahl to take the early release the Vietnamese had offered this seemingly simple-minded child. As the only person who was authorized to accept early release, Hegdahl returned home with 200 names, went to the Paris Peace talks, and told about the mistreatment of the POWs. In the archives of military history, a 19-year old Navy seaman will live as one of the most heroic figures. This teenager never ran out of ideas, but neither did he run out of altitude or airspeed. Through his involvement in a well-defined system, he was able to remain resilient and healthy and to ensure the safe return of many of his fellow POWs.

The need for ideas served as part of the framework the VPOWs created and maintained, a system of strong interpersonal relationships and group affiliation that helped them survive over seven years in captivity and thrive during the years since repatriation. Humor was one of the elements of this system; their commitment to each other and sense of connection were two others. The VPOWs had ideas for helping each other use humor as a weapon for fighting back and as a tool for building cohesion.

The value of taking care of oneself and others is best appreciated in the light of the prisoners' uncertainties and required compliances. Their taking charge of anything allowed a perception of some degree of power. In other words, they found that taking care of themselves and others was a way of coping and exercising some degree of control.

NEVER RUN OUT OF ALTITUDE, AIRSPEED & IDEAS AT THE SAME TIME

SUMMARY

To prevent a disjunction of the self and to find meaning in a situation void of meaning, the VPOWs relied on resources many of them did not know they had:

1. Their internal sense of mirth and humor.
2. Their reliance on one another.
3. Their group interactions all combined to create a system for survival.

Their humor perspective provided the framework for discovering how to cope with their captivity, and their commitment to one another gave them an important perspective about what coping is made of. The role humor can play in bouncing back from adversity, especially when we are linked to others who will help us laugh, seems critical.

Because they were cemented in a strong social structure, they had a buffer against fragmentation of self or of the system. Humor within oneself and with others allows for taking control of a senseless situation and for coping with unexpected or unwelcome changes to our worlds.

These men relied on coping skills related to altitude, airspeed, and ideas not in spite of the crisis but because of it. The Vietnam POWs show us that control is central to individuals' health, their personal benefits, and in the case of the Vietnam POWs, their actual survival. As the boss, you have the responsibility for taking care of yourself during times of change so you can help others; you need to put on your own oxygen masks before you can help anyone else with theirs.

CHAPTER 7

TAKE CHARGE OF CHANGE

Everyone thinks of changing the world, but no one thinks of changing himself.
—TOLSTOY

Mention the word "change," and a large number of people will react with horror, anger, or angst. These people are members of a not-so-elite group of the chronically unraveled. The only change they like jingles in their pockets. In fact, you might be among them. But whether you are or not, chances are some of the members of this group report to you. Steadiness, predictability, and sameness define their areas of comfort.

> In most organizations, change is more like a tornado than a gentle wind.

When they are faced with change, especially unplanned change, they can be seen running to the pharmacy where an entire aisle is stocked with aids for the change phobic. These people don't want or need any of the excitement or new opportunities that may come with experimentation. Things are just fine the way they are, after all. However, the world is not a stagnant place, and stakeholders in the status quo are either experiencing stress, or change initiatives are failing due to a lack of commitment, insufficient training, or confusion about the rationale for change.

John Steinbeck said that "Change comes like a little wind that ruffles the curtains at dawn, and it comes like the stealthy perfume of wildflowers hidden in the grass." Change may come to individuals like that, but in most organizations, the change is more like a tornado than a gentle wind. Demands of the marketplace, the accelerating pace of globalization, innovative technology, and new alliances—all have created needs for bosses to help their people respond quickly and repeatedly to change. Some people thrive on change; they have trouble when things become too predictable or mundane. Those individuals will need your ideas for developing and challenging their talent. However, this chapter is for those bosses who have direct reports who are change averse or "change challenged." This not-so-silent majority would prefer an IRS audit to any change in their software. To help them, therefore, you'll need to understand how to manage change and its impact on people—skills that are among the most fundamental aspects of leadership.

The rapidity of change and the multi-faceted nature of it have created situations for which today's leader has not been prepared. The popular leadership models that for so long provided formulas that equipped leaders to solve business problems are inadequate and insufficient in today's world because they are based on a reality of slower change that no longer exists. Today the orthodoxies of mainstream change endeavors may not be enough to keep your people productive and engaged when they aren't happy about a change that is happening. Yet, in spite of the daunting complexities and uncertainties, leaders are being asked to be the heroes and dynamic geniuses that will keep the doors open and the till full.

> *Popular leadership models are inadequate and insufficient in today's world because they are based on a reality of slower change that no longer exists.*

Managing change is a necessity of leadership; the avoidance of it is its antithesis. For centuries people have understood that the ability to know when to take risks, revolutionize, respond, and adjust separated those who succeeded from those who did not. Hundreds of years ago Dante provided a warning to the leader who might be tempted to think otherwise by describing hell as "the miserable way taken by the sorry souls of those who lived without disgrace or without praise." Unlike hell, however, risk, change aversion, and the mediocrity that both are likely to engender will not last an eternity. Those leaders who do not adjust and adapt both themselves and their organizations will quickly leave the competitive arena. Successful leaders will take their places.

In spite of this looming threat, in 2002 the Center for Creative Leadership estimated that 50 to 70% of change initiatives failed to have the lasting effect they were intended to have. Obviously, leadership in today's economy is not for the fainthearted. Bosses who want to keep star players have to understand change and its impact on those who don't like it, learn ways to handle change themselves, even if they don't like it, and acquire skills for helping others adjust to transitions and stay engaged, even if they don't like it.

The essence of the problem is that for most bosses, managing change is unlike any other managerial task you have ever confronted. You may be able to handle the most complex operational problems, but when it comes to change, the skills and model you use for operational issues just don't work. Unlike managing physical work, during times of change, your task is to manage the *change dynamic*, not the pieces. Like balancing a mobile, you have to attend to all parts of the process instead of concentrating on one piece in isolation. In the throes of change, the critical mission for the boss is to understand how pieces balance one another, how changing one element changes the rest, and how sequencing and pace affect the entire structure.

Bridging the gap between what is happening and what is possible is what change management is all about.

Bridging the gap between what is happening and what is possible is what change management is all about, but to do this, bosses need to understand their own reactions to change and to have the tools for creating a safe environment for experimentation for those in the trenches. Even if you don't personally suffer from the stress of change, you'll need to avoid being a carrier. Companies will require champions of and agents for change who will plan the direction the organization will take, overcome resistance to it, give their direct reports the help they need, and implement the change initiatives. All will take courage and commitment.

UNDERSTAND CHANGE

Centuries ago, a two-part, seemingly contradictory pictogram from the Chinese language indicated an understanding of why people resist change. The bottom part of the symbol meant "opportunity"; the top character meant "danger." To the ancient Chinese, apparently, change included part danger and part opportunity. This ancient symbol helps to explain why people have long resisted change or have become immobilized by it. They have feared it will bring more danger than opportunity. The Chinese knew this centuries ago, and twenty-first century bosses realize it everyday. People don't really fear the change itself; they are frightened about the loss it might bring.

There is no one single way to understand and deal with change; however, researchers have given us some good information for understanding and predicting people's reactions to it. Change, or transition, involves movement, a process that occurs in a series of steps. Sometimes change is instantaneous, and the steps happen almost simultaneously. Certainly September 11th taught us that, but more often it occurs over time and involves a transition from one state to another. Knowing that change involves movement and process suggests that we can expect certain predictable things to occur with people during the change process.

Knowing that change involves movement and process suggests that we can expect certain predictable things to occur with people during the change process.

Researchers and theorists have defined these predictable stages of change or loss. Some describe five stages, others four. Kurt Lewin described three phases: unfreezing, movement, and refreezing. Similar to Lewin's conclusions, my research with the Vietnam POWs indicated that they went through three major stages. Typically, no matter what is involved, we go through these same three stages when a change occurs in our lives: Awareness, adjustment, and readiness to move forward. If we are adaptable and choose to go through the stages in a healthy, purposeful way, we earn the rewards of mastering the challenges of the change. The three stages become our stepping stones to success as we learn to empower ourselves as we move toward triumph.

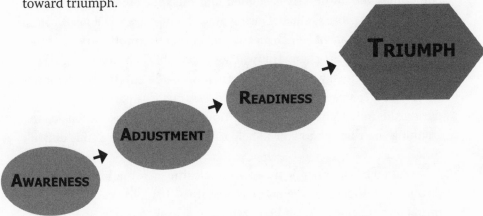

But just as we can learn to empower ourselves and move toward success, we can also learn to be helpless. Angry or resistant, we become victims of change, get stuck in one of the stages, and the stages become a process that leads away from happiness. Bosses who want to keep the best and brightest can benefit from understanding these stages so that they can meet their direct reports wherever they are and help them through the steps that lead to moving on.

Stage I: Awareness

When change comes into our lives, we can react in one of two ways. We can react with denial and resistance, or we can have a sense of challenge and adapt to it.

Similarly, when leading others, you can help them with their own reactions to change by managing your own reactions more successfully. Often you won't be a champion of the change. Circumstances or people above you in the organization will force the change on you and your people. You might be angry; you may be scared; you might even be immobilized. Whatever your initial emotions, you will need to put them aside to do the best thing to help your people with their own feelings. This control over reactions occurs only when you better understand what is going on so that you can go through this stage with a sense of challenge instead of denial.

The single most important thing for you to do is to be consistent, clear, and endlessly repetitious.

Stage I is the period of time when we become aware of the change. Sometimes the awareness is sudden and unexpected; other times it is predicted and more gradual. During Stage I, employees will need you to be a true change agent, which means you will need to motivate your direct reports to accept the change by, whenever possible, offering reassurances and support. Open and honest information is the surest way to reduce anxiety at any stage of the change process, but it is particularly crucial during the initial phase. Explaining timelines, processes, rationale, and anything else that is known will help to ease people through this difficult time.

Too often bosses assume that communicating is something for human resources or upper management to take care of. In reality, communication must be your priority. Your direct reports will look to you for the answers, so try to have as many as you can. If you don't attend to this function of your job, rumors will run rampant, and the grapevine will hum with damaging information. The single most important thing for you to do is to be consistent, clear, and endlessly repetitious.

One of the paradoxes of change is that trust is hardest to establish when it is most needed. In times of change, trust is based on two things:

predictability and consistency, two things that are in short supply during a transition. However, your direct reports will look to you to provide both. As much as possible, they will want you to let them know what to expect and to reassure them that, no matter what happens, things will be okay. Here's how the two reactions can be contrasted:

STAGE I: AWARENESS	
Denial *Behaviors and Feelings*	**Challenge** *Behaviors and Feelings*
Confusion	A willingness to struggle
Focus on the past	Focus on the future
Immobilization	Drive to succeed
Missed meetings or deadlines	Acknowledging the range of feelings
Withdrawal, shutting down	"Wait and see" attitude
Worry & uncertainty	Flexibility
Paralysis	Ability to identify opportunities
Shock & fear	Belief in own abilities
Anger & Frustration, "why me?"	Acceptance of reality
Disorientation	Focus
Shunning friends and family	Closeness to family & friends

Coping Strategies for Stage I

How can you help your direct reports through this stage? Obviously, if they react with a sense of adventure and opportunity, you won't have to do too much except listen to their ideas. However, if they respond with denial, you will need to be more involved. First, make sure you are communicating your acceptance of the change, even if this is somewhat forced and counterfeit in its early stages. Next, ask open-ended questions that will help people discover what they want to do:

- ❏ "What are some options for making this easier?"
- ❏ "What opportunities will we have now that we wouldn't have had before?"
- ❏ "How might you take an active role in this transition?"
- ❏ "What might you gain personally from this change?"

Keep in mind that no matter what you do, this will be a tough time for many people. There is an expression that rings true: "The only people who like change are wet babies." While not universally accurate, there is some veracity in the conclusion that people may want variety and change, but they also want to feel some control over it. When they don't, they are often unhappy.

The length of time it takes most people to go through this stage will vary greatly. Some will breeze through in a matter of days, but more typically, people will need a few weeks to let the reality sink in. If people are mired here for more than two months, there may be significant issues at play that will require more help than a boss can give. In those rare cases, asking the direct report to get help from the Employee Assistance Plan or another clinical professional might be advisable. Winston Churchill offered some sage advice for people going through Stage I: "If you're going through hell, keep going."

Stage II: Adjustment

Usually by Stage II people are finally ready to accept that the change is not going away. This is the period during which people accept that the change is unavoidable, especially if they want to stay employed, pay their mortgage, and get their kids' braces paid for. However, they will either build obstacles to resist the changes and reject personal responsibility, or they will cope and explore opportunities. Even if they have not skated through the first stage too well, once several months have passed, people start to live in harmony with their changed world. They will still need your help, however, to make wise decisions to reinvent their worlds, or they will be tempted to retreat from coping.

STAGE II: ADJUSTMENT	
Resistance *Behaviors and Feelings*	**Adapting** *Behaviors and Feelings*
Confusion	Curiosity about future
Anxiety	Willingness to confront change
Withdrawal	Building relationships
Exaggerated need to control	Ability to live 1 day at a time
Shifting of responsibility	Development of responsibility
"Arguing" with new reality	Courage to understand change
Commitment to "go it alone"	Willingness to ask for help
Resisting new ideas	Openness to learning
Refusing to try new ideas	Willingness to take risks
Tunnel vision on the one solution	Willingness to explore
Inability to feel joy	Ability to celebrate success

Coping Strategies for Stage II

Adjusting to a new reality or a new set of realities requires the development of new skills or the honing of skills so they can be applied to a new set of circumstances. Specifically, your direct reports will need your help with problem solving, relationships, and flexibility, the same three skills that you will need for yourself to maintain altitude, airspeed, and ideas.

Problem Solving is the ability to deal directly with the difficult situations we face and to make positive changes to resolve them. Effective problem solving involves critical thinking, a global perspective, strategic planning, and the ability to anticipate consequences. When you eagerly probe for understanding, go beyond the obvious, and prioritize effectively, you will help your direct reports see the future as open and malleable. Together you will be able to paint a credible picture of opportunities and possibilities and to communicate your enthusiasm for making them happen. Here are some ways you can help others cope with change by improving their problem solving abilities:

❑ Encourage people to solve problems as soon as they are aware of them.

❑ Ask your direct reports to separate problems so that they are manageable. Put each in one sentence by saying, "The problem is...."

❑ Separate emotions from the problem. Decide what is right, not who is right.

❑ Help people determine their desired outcome. Start with the end in mind.

❑ Brainstorm. List a variety of creative and practical solutions.

❑ Don't let them get trapped into thinking that there is only one solution to any problem. See options as having pros and cons rather than being "right" or "wrong."

Effective communication is the single most important ability that will help your direct reports build relationships and share thoughts and feelings with you and each other in order to promote mutual understanding, even during difficult circumstances. Those who welcome closeness will have developed a supportive social fabric in each area of their lives. When they combine communication and closeness, they will have the necessary tools for building the relationships that will help them stay connected and supported during difficult times, but this connection doesn't happen automatically.

> *Mental agility has another important payoff: It stimulates creativity.*

On the contrary, the closeness that engenders effective communication relies on a willingness to listen, the capacity to convey respect for others' ideas, and a genuine interest in people. When people exhibit these behaviors that make them feel close to each other, they will have the trust and safety to engage in fun, laughter, and play. A sense of what is funny, or mirth, has its basis in the individual, but the true value of humor manifests itself in interpersonal associations.

Making relationships a priority, building time into our lives for the people who are important to us, laughing together, and having fun with each other all create interactions that are characterized by joy and fun. Sharing our feelings and concerns enhances these relationships and encourages more closeness. An upward spiral of cohesion and connection starts to build on itself when we communicate with one another in our attempts to focus on the positive. As a result, we are better able to deal with the stressors in our lives. You can't force these kinds of things, however. You can only create an environment in which they are allowed to flourish. During times of change, the wise boss does well to realize that people will need to spend more time building a sense of connection to people both at home and at work.

Flexibility is the degree of organization in our lives and the extent to which we feel comfortable with unstructured and unpredictable situations. Life is unpredictable, so our responses to the problems it creates need to be too. Flexibility is one way to make that happen. Mental agility has another important payoff: It stimulates creativity. Being open to a variety of creative and imaginative alternatives allows us to avoid getting trapped into thinking there is only one resolution. When you encourage your direct reports to avoid rigidity in their thinking, to experiment with innovation, and to seek the input of others, they can become more open to new ways of solving problems.

Once you help people quit fighting the currents and learn to flow with them, they can approach decision making with new dexterity and energy. No one can control change, yet if we're not careful, it will control us. When people are forced to adjust to new, uninvited changes, feeling out of control is a common, normal response.

As the Vietnam POWs taught us, finding humor in difficult situations is one way of controlling what we can control, even if we can't have power over the events that required us to marshal our coping behaviors in the first place. As the previous chapter explained, much evidence exists to support the idea that humor is a determinant of resilience. People have learned to rely on it, not in spite of crisis but *because* of it. Becoming aware of the value of using humor to expand coping behaviors can increase our understanding of the powerful role humor and laughter can play in helping us bounce back from the hardships that unwanted changes often bring. Then, consciously and actively working to help others find humor in their daily lives can help them feel better until things get better. When we use humor to tackle problems effectively, build strong relationships, and explore new ideas, we are doing what we can do to turn challenges into opportunities. Even though the second stage of adjustment may take your direct reports two or three months, with your help, they will be equipped to move forward.

Stage III: Moving Forward

Stage III is the stage during which most people are truly ready to identify with new goals and clearly focus on how to reach them. They have experienced the transformation of transition and are ready to commit. Reaching this stage is not automatic, however. Sometimes people get stuck in a previous stage, and the change will not be successful for them.

Coping Strategies for Stage III:

Your primary responsibility during Stage III is to offer ongoing support. If you see regression, you will need to determine what is going on. Usually a regression in behavior is a sign that the person never really coped with the change. There might be an attempt at moving forward, but if you sense that there's no real progress, this might be an indication that the person needs more help.

Weeks or even months of progress can be compromised if a person can't truly move on with the altered reality. Sometimes too many changes that come too close together can cause people to regress. At other times, changes in the personal lives of your direct reports can seemingly gang up on them. Whatever the cause, the boss' reaction is the same.

Determine where they are, and then offer them the guidance and support they need, provided they will let you. Even if you're the best boss in the world, you can't protect your people from unexpected events that rock their worlds. The best you can do is to develop the skills for helping them when this kind of change does occur—and planning change every chance you get.

STAGE III: MOVING FORWARD	
Regression *Behaviors and Feelings*	**Commitment** *Behaviors and Feelings*
Inability to cope with change	Adaptation to the new world
Powerlessness	Acceptance of reality
Sense of failure	Sense of accomplishment
Feelings of helplessness	Sense of control & mastery
Doubt	Confidence
Focus on loss and regret	Feelings of satisfaction
Confirmation of regression	Evidence of personal growth
Inability to find purpose in life	Ability to find meaning in life
Incapacity for experiencing joy	Willingness to experience joy
Angst, uneasiness & distress	Achievement of peace

WHENEVER POSSIBLE, PLAN CHANGE

One of the things that 9/11 taught companies is that you can't always plan for events that will impact the way you do business. Air travel suddenly became difficult; industries that relied on travel unexpectedly suffered losses; and out of the blue, doing business abroad had new challenges. The fact that your passport photo is hideous is now the least of your worries. No one could have predicted these changes, but companies that were experienced in planning change had the tools to quickly respond.

Organizational development and improvement depend on the ability to initiate, anticipate, and respond to change, something that most people are not particularly good at. Whether planned or unplanned, when change occurs, the leader is called upon to navigate the waters of uncertainty, an arduous but sometimes exciting venture. By constantly tying short-term actions to long-term goals, you can balance the pressures of today with the needs of tomorrow. This does not happen automatically.

The first step is to align the company's mission, vision, values, and goals with the activities of your direct reports. One of the most important questions you can ask is, "What is our business and what should it be?" This leads to setting objectives, developing strategies and plans, and the making of today's decisions for tomorrow's results.

When you and your direct reports see the entire business, make decisions, balance short and long-term objectives, and allocate resources to realize them, you will be the ones who determine the company's direction, and you will take an important step toward overcoming resistance.

MANAGE RESISTANCE

People resist change because they fear danger, challenge, or annoyance. Usually change involves loss, even if it's just the loss of predictability or familiarity. Change often creates emotional overload and chaos, two of the most potent ingredients in the recipe for resistance. Therefore, people frequently oppose change for the following reasons:

❑ They think it is unnecessary or are not confident it will work.

❑ They fear personal loss.

❑ They had no input into the decision to make the change.

❑ They perceive a loss of control.

❏ They feel threatened and fear they won't be able to perform well in the new situation.

❏ They just like things the way they are.

Preparedness for resistance is the main requirement for successfully managing it. Bosses frequently focus their attention on the abstract process of the change instead of carefully listening to their direct reports about the practical problems that they will encounter in their altered worlds. One of the critical mistakes that bosses make in change initiatives is they seemingly overlook the fact that change usually requires some new behaviors, new ways of thinking and responding, and a new set of practices or protocols. This does not imply that you will try to "convert" anyone to seeing the value of the change; rather it means that you can be responsive and empathic to the fact that when people become aware of change they are often angry, scared, immobilized, and scattered.

Aventis Pharmaceutical recently faced a change initiative. They needed to implement a learning management system (LMS) globally in both the Research and Development organization and in the clinical groups within the Commercial Operations organization. After only one year, the LMS had achieved widespread acceptance within the organization and has been implemented. How did they do it?

Traditionally at Aventis managers and staff were responsible for tracking training to meet regulatory requirements. The LMS was a valuable improvement because it fosters consistency in tracking, and it delivers and manages training throughout the organization. The goal was to have each department define its individual training requirements within the LMS and eventually own the maintenance of the related content. The hope was that LMS users would learn to appreciate the value of the new system because it creates a situation wherein employees are more empowered to influence when, where, and what they learn.

Aventis did some smart things to launch their new system that can work as a protocol for other companies streamlining the change process:

❏ Let people know what you're trying to do. Have an achievable goal in mind and clearly communicate it to everyone who will be affected. If lack of communication is the problem, the solution is simple. Through one-on-one discussions, memos, group presentations, or reports, disseminate the facts. If your relationships with your direct reports were characterized by mutual respect and credibility to start with, your willingness to be candid during change will go a long way in reducing resistance.

❏ Buy in to the change. What if you don't? Fake it. If the change is going to happen, and there's nothing you can do about it, the biggest favor you can do your direct reports is to keep your concerns to yourself. Voice your reservations to your boss, the Board of Directors, your friends, your spouse, or your minister, but spare your direct reports. They need your help; you can't rely on them for theirs.

❏ Gather as much data as possible. Let the facts speak for themselves and then deliver this information to everyone whose life will be affected.

❏ Involve others early in the process. Resisting a change that they played a role in creating is difficult for most people. If possible, use a committee or team to help with the implementation. Some problems can only be solved by those in the trenches. As Taoist sage Lao Tzu put it, "Learn from the people. Plan with the people...When the task is accomplished, the people all remark, 'We have done it ourselves.'"

❏ Listen to feedback and consider concerns. There are no more frequent opportunities to use the GLAD Communication Method than during times of change. The absolute last thing your direct reports need is a boss who in essence says, "Tell me what you need, and I'll tell you how to get along without it." People are likely to have subjective, illogical reactions to unwanted changes, so they will need you to listen empathically and help them sort out what they need to do. Remember that it usually isn't what you say. The best sermons are lived, not preached, and the most important words you say will be whispered, not shouted.

❏ Create a safe learning environment for experimenting with the new procedure. Consider the lines from Winnie-the-

Pooh: "Here is Edward Bear, coming downstairs now, bump, bump, bump, on the back of his head behind Christopher Robin. It is, as far as he knows, the only way of coming downstairs, but sometimes he feels that there really is another way, if only he could stop bumping for a moment and think of it." Your charge will be to help your direct reports quit bumping for a moment so they can explore new ways to think of a better way to function.

❑ Concentrate on confronting problems squarely and learn from failures. Then, everyone can focus on identifying and removing obstacles to everyone's success.

When possible, measure outcomes and report progress. Even if people have initially defied the change, once they understand that the new conditions are helping the organization, they are more likely to accept that they stand to profit too. Whenever possible, reinforce the change by demonstrating the relationship between their behavior and organizational success. Peter Senge offered five characteristics of organizations that can align effective behaviors, learn from mistakes, and succeed:

1. Everyone agrees on a shared vision.
2. People discard their old ways.
3. People think of all organizational processes as parts of a system of interrelationships.
4. People communicate without fear of criticism or punishment.
5. People sublimate personal agendas in order to achieve the organization's shared vision.

Give people as much power as possible to control issues that touch their worlds. When people know the 4 P's of change, the **P**urpose of the change, the **P**icture of what it will look like, a **P**lan for going forward, and the **P**art they will play in the new system, they move toward success.

When a major change occurs, go back to the accountability chart and discuss what decisions each person will have in the new world. If people feel that they have a say, they will be committed to results. However, empowerment does not mean abandonment, and delegation does not mean abdication. Giving people permission to do something differently is not helpful if they are unable to do it, so delegate wisely.

TAKE CHARGE OF CHANGE

SUMMARY

Henry David Thoreau said, "Things do not change. We do."

People get attached to the status quo, even when it doesn't work anymore, isn't good for anyone, or doesn't make sense in any sane way. Fear of the unknown immobilizes many. However, when bosses don't change, they endure the consequences of lost opportunities; when they don't help their direct reports change, they suffer the penalties of lost people.

What should a boss do?

1. Understand change.

2. Plan the direction it will take.

3. Overcome resistance.

Implementing change initiatives is part of you making the organization's vision a reality, and plays a role in you becoming the leader no one wants to leave, not even during adversity or transition.

Successful bosses are the ones who can provide their direct reports with the insight, motivation, and opportunity to grow as they manage the process of change. Leaders do not just lead change, however. They must also influence the priorities of multiple stakeholders, align resources, and identify short and long-term consequences of failing to implement the new initiative.

CHAPTER 8

COACH A WINNING TEAM

The way a team plays as a whole determines its success. You may have the greatest bunch of individual stars in the world, but if they don't play together, the club won't be worth a dime.
—BABE RUTH

The words "teams" and "meetings" often cause excessive blinking and curious looks of pain to cross the faces of many executives, implying that nausea is following closely behind. Even though these same people might have fond memories of sports team membership, they haven't transferred those fuzzy feelings to the corporate world. In an attempt to understand this phenomenon, I asked one executive about his perceptions of meetings and teamwork in his organization. He said, "When it comes to people trying to work together around here, when all is said and done, there's a lot more said than done."

This simple phrase sums up both the frustration with using teams and many individuals' bad experiences with them. For the most part, people excel in organizations, not because they have been good team players but because they have been such strong solo contributors. To require these same people suddenly to develop esprit de corps is not only daunting; it is intimidating and more than a little confusing. But this doesn't stop many companies from scheduling expensive team experiences that offer a variety of unpleasant situations, often in outdoor settings, that are designed specifically to advance cohesion. They don't. They just bother people, cost copious amounts of money, and keep people from doing what it takes to tackle the tough issues related to building collaboration within a group of people who have always been fiercely self-sufficient.

> *For the most part, people excel in organizations, not because they have been good team players but because they have been such strong solo contributors.*

To further complicate the situation, individual efforts are usually compensated more directly than team contributions. Yet, as individuals move to the higher levels of responsibility in the company, their success is not only determined more often by the work of their subordinates; it is also more frequently influenced by their abilities to work as an executive; and each factor of success is directly related to interpersonal team-building skills. Although "teamwork" is a somewhat global and abstract term that generally means everyone pulling in the same direction, actual "team building" is more specific.

Team building requires bosses to do five things: decide whether you really need a team, encourage cohesive efforts, align efforts to accomplish tasks, have better meetings, and help others resolve their differences.

DECIDE WHETHER YOU NEED A TEAM

The first question you need to answer is, "Do we need a team or even a meeting?" If one person has the requisite resources, knowledge, and experiences, and buy in from others is not important, an individual should make the decision or carry out the task. On the other hand, when no one person can make the decision or accomplish the task, or when the outcome will affect others whose support is crucial, a team effort is indicated. But keep this in mind. Creating a team is not your goal. It is a means for achieving an organizational goal that people working alone cannot accomplish.

The first question you need to answer is, "Do we need a team or even a meeting?"

The overriding question you must answer is, "Do we need a team or a collection of solo contributors?" If you need solo performers to operate as a team occasionally, you will have a different point of view than if you truly need a cohesive, high performing team that cannot function without the collaboration of the other members. The principles are the same, but the standard to which participants will need to model them will differ.

If you decide you truly need a team, your first challenge is to see teams as dynamic, living systems that change as quickly as you understand them. The next step is to provide an awareness that teams are process-oriented, synergetic, and environmentally dependent entities that meet to accomplish that which no one member could accomplish alone.

Understand Interdependence on Teams

As the Vietnam POWs showed us, teamwork is the fuel that allows ordinary people to achieve extraordinary results, but for centuries this was a misunderstood concept because people thought that dissecting, reducing, and taking things apart was the best way to learn about it. Scientists examined an entity by analyzing each individual component, further splitting the elements so they could scrutinize the smallest parts of it. This way of looking at the world was popular until the twentieth century. Then a new approach to understanding began to surface: the systems approach.

In 1952, Ludwig Von Bertalanffy, a theoretical biologist, identified a new approach, General Systems Theory. This theory allowed a new way to think about and study the interactive and dynamic alterations of a living phenomenon, like a team. A system is an organized set of interrelated and interacting parts that maintain their own balance amid the influences of the environment.

> *Teamwork is people working together, even when they are apart.*

A team is such a system. To use a classic definition, a team is "a small number of people with complimentary skills who are committed to a common purpose, performance goals, and approach for which they hold themselves mutually accountable." When taken apart, a system, such as a team, loses its interaction and essential properties. Explaining one part of the team's process without taking the entire structure into account does not give an accurate picture. Teamwork is people working together, even when they are apart.

In spite of the obvious interconnectedness of a team, analyzing team process traditionally involved a division of the process into smaller, more manageable parts, such as roles, norms, size, and leadership. This fragmenting allowed an in-depth look at the different forces that take place within a team; but since teams are complex, ever-changing structures, reducing the process to individual elements and treating them as though they were independent, constant, and static prevented a clear understanding of how dynamic the team process is.

The interconnected and interrelating aspects of a team cause the members to be *interdependent*. Interdependence means that team members can accomplish something as a whole that would be difficult or impossible for a single individual to achieve. In other words, team members may divide the tasks, but in doing so, they are often able to double the success. However, this accomplishment can only occur when members can rely on each other to fulfill their roles and responsibilities.

Understanding *how* teams operate rather than merely concentrating on *what* they do gives a better picture of the wholeness of teams as systems. No one part of a system can be understood unless it is viewed within the context of the entire system.

See Your Team as a Living System

A team is a system with a collection of parts that interact with each other to function as a whole. If something is made up of a number of parts that do not interact, and the arrangement of these parts is irrelevant, this is a pile of materials rather than a system. For example, a pile of bricks is a pile of bricks whether we add to it or subtract from it. Cutting it in half gives two piles of bricks and adding to it yields a bigger pile of bricks. Essentially, however, the mound of material remains a mound of material; conversely, cutting a car in half does not produce two smaller cars.

Combined, the team members can do things that no one of them could do separately.

In fact, if the best parts of each type of automobile were determined, could the world's best car be manufactured by collecting each of these parts and putting them together? Taking the engine from one type of car, a transmission from another model, and a carburetor from yet another would not combine to create a system that would work. The parts would not be compatible, and they would not operate to make a functioning machine, much less a superlative mode of transportation. Similarly, cutting an elephant in half does not give you two smaller elephants; it gives you two large, dead hunks.

Teams are even more complicated; they are *living* systems. Each person on the team is a separate part of the system, but the effect of the interactions among the members is more than the sum of the parts. The synergy among the members is the result of the dynamic relationships they create by constantly defining and redefining themselves, their behavior, and the functions of the team. Consequently, combined, the team members can do things that no one of them could do separately.

ENCOURAGE COHESION

Business expert Ken Blanchard said, "None of us is as smart as all of us." This means that 1 + 1 = 3, or a team is more than the sum of its parts. Synergy occurs when the team's performance or accomplishments surpass the capabilities of the individual team members. It is the bonus that occurs when things work together harmoniously. In other words, the team's unique combination of talents, knowledge, and experience is greater than the sum of the individual contributions.

The vitality of one individual can spur others on when their own energy wanes.

The members can align the efforts of each person to create a synergy that goes beyond the capacities that any one person could achieve. The ideas of one member often trigger a response from another person that neither would have thought of independently. Further, the vitality of one individual can spur others on when their own energy wanes.

Synergy can take either a physical or a mental form. Think of a symphony. No one instrument can create the harmony or brilliance of an entire orchestra. In a well-conducted performance, no one instrument overpowers the others. All are needed. Similarly, the development of a team is a kind of aligning during which a commonality of direction emerges, and individuals' energies harmonize. Systems theorist Peter Senge wrote that a resonance occurs that is "like the coherent light of a laser rather than the incoherent and shattered light of a light bulb." This laser focus of efforts creates a commonality of purpose, a shared vision, and an understanding of how to complement one another's efforts.

Even though all teams share some common ground, each team is unique because each team member is unique. The team, therefore, becomes a system of people, each bringing to the experience an individualized genetic make-up, a personal life history, a combination of traits, talents, differing values, and attitudes, and a singular view of the world. Adding the input of these individuals, however, still does not give a clear picture of what the team is or will do because each person is constantly changing due to the association with the team; and the team is continuously reacting in response to each person's membership.

The team's members will interact to create the team, a creation that will be like no other. The members' behaviors, their verbal and nonverbal interactions, their strengths, their weaknesses, their insights, and their talents will not only separate this team from all others; but it will also distinguish a particular team's interactions today from this same team's interactions tomorrow.

The team's synergy is a source of energy that gives structure to the system, thereby reducing disorder. When people form a team that is characterized by synergy, cohesion and often even a desire for *conformity* are natural outcomes. This tendency is neither good nor bad, just predictable. The outcome, however, can be negative if groupthink or undue pressures to conform prevail. Certainly the Bay of Pigs invasion during Kennedy's administration and the Challenger tragedy gave us concrete examples of the horrific outcomes that can occur when people too readily jump on the groupthink bandwagon.

Cohesive teams usually enjoy low turnover and high participation because members desire continuation of the team and its commitment to goal accomplishment.

When not excessive, however, the desire to be identified with others is positive. Cohesion is the "glue" that causes the members to remain with a team even when there are pressures or influences to leave it. Sometimes the personal attraction among the participants contributes to cohesion, but often there is a satisfaction in achieving a goal that could not otherwise have been attained that causes the cohesion to develop.

Cohesive teams usually enjoy low turnover and high participation because members desire continuation of the team and its commitment to goal accomplishment. When trust, support, and affection exist among the participants, there is room for personal growth, even if that means an occasional expression of hostility, dissatisfaction, or frustration.

Another characteristic of a team that will influence its success is its size. As teams grow larger, the system becomes more complex. The interdependence is there but less apparent. Cohesion tends to be weaker, and morale is likely to be lower in larger teams than in comparable smaller ones. In general, people like to talk rather than listen in a group. Smaller teams provide this opportunity.

The ideal size of a work team is usually five to seven members. Any fewer, and there often aren't enough people to share the responsibilities; any more and satisfaction and cohesion may be compromised. Team size is directly related to communication networks. As the size of the team increases, the network begins to bog down. Larger teams tend to produce lower levels of satisfaction and weaker interpersonal relations among participants because people have fewer opportunities to interact with each other. The smart boss includes only those people who are critical to the success of the project, thereby strengthening the cohesion among the members and using wisely the time of those who are critical to the success of the team's undertakings.

What does all this mean for the boss? If people enjoy opportunities to work with others (not everyone does), and you can create situations for them to do so by aligning their efforts, you may be able to take yet another step toward retaining top performers. Top players want to play on a winning team, so create that team for and with them.

HELP TEAMS GET RESULTS

Creating opportunities for team members to work together is one of the requirements for building a strong team. Helping them realize exceptional results is the other. You won't be able to do either or to improve team performance unless you know what the members are thinking and feeling. The surest way to find answers to your questions is simply to ask. You'll be most motivated to spend time on this when your team is stuck, but often that will be too late. A more proactive approach is to do some team building to help them leverage their strengths when things are going well.

One way to begin the process is to use an anonymous survey that includes a scale from 1 to 10. Ask each person to examine the team's functions related to trust, commitment, accountability, results, decision making, problem solving, conflict resolution, communication, leadership, goal setting, and meetings. (See next page.) You can average the numbers and present them to the group during a team meeting.

The survey results will indicate that one or two of these are strengths and three or four are the most critical or the most underdeveloped. When everyone knows this information, the members can begin the process of leveraging strengths and overcoming weaknesses. When each team member commits to an action, you are on your way to improvement.

Team members can experience anxiety from a variety of sources, but the causes can usually be tied to either task accomplishment or faulty interpersonal relationships. When task issues are the problem, the survey results will typically indicate that the team is low in goal setting, accountability, conflict resolution, and purposeful meetings. People will

TEAM FUNCTION ANALYSIS

On a scale from 1-10, with 10 meaning you strongly agree and 1 meaning you strongly disagree, rate the following team functions:

Trust	1	2	3	4	5	6	7	8	9	10
Commitment	1	2	3	4	5	6	7	8	9	10
Accountability	1	2	3	4	5	6	7	8	9	10
Results	1	2	3	4	5	6	7	8	9	10
Decision Making/Problem Solving	1	2	3	4	5	6	7	8	9	10
Conflict Resolution	1	2	3	4	5	6	7	8	9	10
Communication	1	2	3	4	5	6	7	8	9	10
Leadership	1	2	3	4	5	6	7	8	9	10
Goal Setting	1	2	3	4	5	6	7	8	9	10
Meetings	1	2	3	4	5	6	7	8	9	10

disclose that they are worried about setting priorities, managing time, coordinating efforts and distributing work. When goals are unclear, or when members can't agree on the goal, strain is the inevitable outcome. Therefore, setting concrete, specific, measurable goals not only contributes to task completion; it also helps to circumvent one of the main causes of the tension and sets the stage for clarifying how to distribute the work.

Define Areas of Accountability

Perhaps the most significant cause of problems for teams is that members literally don't know what they or other members are doing or should be doing. Clear lines of responsibility have not been drawn; people don't communicate; and individual accountability has not been established. This lack of understanding creates barriers among team members that significantly impedes efficient and effective teamwork, but with the right kind of help, team members can learn methods for removing these obstacles.

One of the best tools you can use to help a team overcome some of the discord so members can get back on track is to have a candid discussion about areas of accountability for task accomplishment and decision making. Modifying the Accountability Chart introduced in Chapter Five, you can guide the members to discuss exactly what they need, want, and expect from one another (See next page).

The goal of accountability charting is to help the members operate more effectively by clarifying each team member's role, responsibilities, and expectations. Charting helps the group and each individual by providing appreciation of the functions of team members in the achievement of organizational goals, clarifying appropriate participation in problem solving and decision making, generating relevant and timely communication, and identifying the right people for work assignments, projects, meetings and task forces.

It also helps people learn how not to step on each other's toes and how not to assume someone else will take care of a particular task. In short, accountability charting reduces friction among members by improving the way the team operates, by defining responsibilities for work, and by opening communication channels about the work that needs to be done. Then, you will be able to make sure you are using the time of each team member wisely when you do meet to discuss issues.

TEAM ACCOUNTABILITY CHART

Directions: Developing an Accountability Chart is a two-phase process: First, in pre-work, each team member lists and analyzes his or her major responsibilities and roles. Then, working together, they share their list with team members, discuss them and reach team consensus. This will be done for all team members, including the team leader.

A = Authority to make decisions
R = Responsibility for the decision/task
N = Notification—Courtesy only
C = Consultation—must OK before proceeding

Major Decision/ Task	Name	Name	Name	Name

CONDUCT BETTER MEETINGS

Ask executives about their biggest waste of time, and the answer will usually be emails or meetings. In spite of both being effective modes of communicating certain kinds of information, both can be huge time drains. As I mentioned in the beginning of the chapter, unless you need the ideas of many or require buy in from the other stakeholders, make the decision yourself.

On the other hand, if you think the meeting is essential to the team's operation, making the best use of everyone's time can pay enormous dividends. There are entire books written on the subject of holding better meetings, but in a nutshell most bosses most of the time can improve by encouraging better communication, setting an agenda, identifying a timekeeper and naming a "process checker," establishing a "parking lot," avoiding giving your opinions first, appointing a devil's advocate and starting and ending on time.

Encourage Better Communication

Robust discussion is not something that happens automatically among members of a team. It has to start with you. Are you willing to put issues on the table and engage in frankness and straightforwardness? If you aren't, it's unlikely that you'll encourage it, yet a high level of candor is critical to your team's creative problem solving. Too often bosses make harmony their goal. After all, it's more pleasant. But truth needs to win over harmony in every team discussion. Only by you pulling it out of your direct reports will this happen, however.

Discussing with others in the organization what was said in a team meeting usually has grim results.

Do you invite questions and encourage dissent, even about your ideas? When roles, egos, rank, and titles are checked at the door, the team will have a chance to get to the core of the issues through testing ideas and experimenting with new approaches. On the other hand, if discussion is constrained and politicized, people may avoid confrontation, but they will also avoid solving the problem. What can you do? Invite multiple viewpoints and encourage questioning. The discussions in your team meetings should not turn into a combat sport for some and a humiliation for others, but they should put the touchy subjects on the table so that they can be resolved.

Another word of caution: What happens in the team meeting stays in the team meeting. Discussing with others in the organization what was said in a meeting usually has grim results. Things are taken out of context, rumors are fueled, and discord is likely. In other words, disagree behind closed doors but present a united front, especially to direct reports.

Set the Agenda, Have a Timeline & Stick to It

Each person on the team should have a chance to submit items for the team's agenda, but this needs to be done ahead of time. If it is your meeting, usually your assistant will take responsibility for emailing the team members to solicit agenda items. A deadline for this is critical. With rare exceptions, if the item isn't submitted by the deadline, usually the day before the meeting, it goes on the agenda for the next meeting. Once you see the kinds of things team members want to discuss, you can allocate time for that issue.

The boss or member who called the meeting makes the decision about the length of time the group will spend discussing each topic, but another team member, the timekeeper, should actually be the enforcer of the times. Each member should assume this responsibility at different times so that responsibilities for timeliness become a shared responsibility and a team norm. When there are two minutes remaining in the time allocated for a given topic, the timekeeper can warn the team that they need to wrap things up. If the team has not reached any resolution of the issue, it goes into the "parking lot," a list that captures non-agenda items.

The Parking Lot

In its simplest terms, the parking lot is a flip chart that is set up away from the other flip charts, PowerPoint screen, and other central parts of the meeting room. When a topic comes up that is not on the agenda, the process checker or person who brought it up writes it on the parking lot page. Often you will need to suggest that the person write it there because people usually like to discuss their issues as soon as they think of them. However, this moves the group off the tasks of the day and siphons energy that is needed for the current concern. Establishing the parking lot does two things. First, it captures the problems and questions so they are not forgotten. Second, it communicates an eagerness to hear the ideas and opinions of each member at the appropriate time.

The Process Checker

One of the problems in meetings is individual members tend to be too talkative or too quiet. Neither extreme is good for the team; therefore, the process checker is a member whose job is to comment on how much or how little people are talking. For instance, the process checker might say, "Mike, we haven't heard any ideas from you." Or, "Susan, let's hear from some of the other members." When people know others are paying attention to their role in the meeting, they tend to be more productive in their discussions. When the topic strays into an area that is not on the agenda, the process checker or person who called the meeting can suggest putting the issue in the "parking lot."

The Boss Speaks Last

The surest way for you to encourage groupthink and currying favor is to let people know what you want them to say. Then, wasting no time, each team member will take a turn being the echo, telling you exactly what you want to hear. As harmonious as this seems, it is not the reason for a meeting, and it's not the best way to solve problems.

Instead, if you make one of the Rules of Engagement be that you will speak last, team members will learn that you don't intend to voice an opinion until they have exhausted their ideas and opinions. Only then, and only when something has been missed, should you add new ideas. If you think this is a waste of time and aren't really interested in hearing the perceptions of the team, ask yourself if you really need a meeting or team input on this issue. If you don't, once again, make the decision yourself and save everyone some valuable time.

Appoint a "Devil's Advocate"

If you sense during the meeting that members are too quickly jumping on the bandwagon and too eagerly agreeing with each other, call their attention to the fact and, if necessary, appoint a "devil's advocate," a member who assumes the responsibility of questioning assumptions and challenging consensus. Usually people won't do this automatically since it may seem impolite or non-teamy, but if you appoint someone to do the dirty work of questioning, the team members will quickly conclude that you don't intend to buy the first idea they have, and you want a thorough investigation of alternatives. Only then are you likely to avoid groupthink.

Start and End On Time

As self-evident as this idea is, you'd be surprised how seldom it is followed. Frequently the group waits for one or two stragglers. Then, because of a late start, the meeting runs over the allotted time. Both build resentment. The sharp boss knows that one of the surest ways to foster respect is to value people's time. One could argue that the team members are on company time, so it doesn't matter, but most executives know this isn't that simple. People have deadlines that they have to meet, so if a meeting runs over, they end up staying later than usual or taking work home. Neither builds good rapport among the team members or between the boss and the direct reports. Above all, be on time yourself. Walk through the door right on time and begin immediately. You will send a loud and clear message that time is of the essence for them and you, and you have no tolerance for tardiness.

HELP MEMBERS RESOLVE DIFFERENCES

Team membership provides a way for relieving pressure because distributing responsibilities and talking with others who share our concerns can relieve tension and reduce stress. Research tells us that groups make more daring decisions than a person working alone would, primarily because of the shared responsibility and blame if something goes wrong. Sometimes individuals can do their best work in a team setting, but this won't happen automatically. Your direct reports will need for you to model the way and help them balance a concern for the task with a focus on relationships.

Not all tension is related to goal accomplishment; often teams experience problems with interpersonal relationships. Your willingness to convey respect for each member, foster trust, and encourage two-way communication will set the stage for team members to adopt these behaviors in their interactions with one another.

We are drawn to groups because of our needs for affection, control, and inclusion. In work situations there is often little choice about joining a team, but this reality does not imply that we won't still have these same needs. When these needs are not met or when they are threatened, strain is the outcome. Of course, agonizing about completing the task can be a source of interpersonal conflict, but frequently other behaviors cause dissention. Only by knowing what behaviors others want us to do more of or less of can we know how to improve our involvement on the team.

The key to positive interpersonal relationships among team members is feeling the freedom to express both positive and negative emotions. This liberty causes the participants to experience camaraderie that is unavailable except in team settings, even when the expressed feelings would be classified as negative. Anger, like tension, is usually seen as something destructive, something to be avoided. But when it is managed, anger can provide the energy that helps the team move toward action, to mobilize it into action. Healthy teamwork depends on the ability of the participants to give accurate feedback to each other, even when this feedback is negative. Anger helps to do that.

> *Healthy teamwork depends on the ability of the participants to give accurate feedback to each other, even when this feedback is negative.*

Although anger is the emotion that prompts us to act, it is not usually the first emotion that we feel. Typically, something causes the anger. We tend to ignore the first emotion and report the anger that follows. For instance, if the team is being distracted, not focusing on the task, and generally just wasting time, a member might become frustrated or impatient; but instead of reporting these emotions to the team, he or she will wait until anger has taken over before saying anything.

Ideally, members would spontaneously report emotions as they felt them, but most people are not good at or comfortable with this. Furthermore, most people view conflict as negative, so in trying to avoid controversy, they will put off reporting negative feelings until anger forces the issue. At this point the team is motivated to resolve the problem but only if the members have effectively addressed their emotions. Misdirected anger has a way of sabotaging the team's efforts and causing more disagreements.

Conflict can occur anytime desires, intentions, values, or opinions are in opposition to those of another team member. Conflicts are not "bad," but we avoid them because we fear the adverse conditions that may occur if the controversy is not managed constructively. Resolving disagreements in groups can be more complicated than individuals resolving disputes because there is an audience involved. Face-saving, embarrassment, pride, and divided loyalties play roles when several people are affected by the struggle.

What should you do? Put the issues on the table and have people talk about them. When conflict does occur among team members, it should be settled as soon as possible, because if it is not negotiated to a conclusion, it will shadow all phases of the discussion process and will interfere with the team reaching its goal. This can be particularly troublesome when the team is trying to operate under time restraints. When clashes occur, the team members, as a rule, react in one of five ways: withdrawing, suppressing, abusing power, compromise, or collaboration. Only collaboration that leads to consensus is in the team's best interest.

Consensus does not mean total agreement. Neither does it imply that members have capitulated.

Collaboration or problem solving is the recommended course of action. When teams take the time to dig deeply into issues to find underlying concerns, a win/win result becomes more likely. Fully exploring alternatives and attempting to find solutions that satisfy all concerned create an environment in which talents and expertise are recognized and utilized. Collaboration that leads to consensus is ideal, but the process is time consuming, a factor that causes many teams to opt for a quicker fix. But when all members of the team will be required to implement the group's decision, the time is well spent.

Consensus does not mean total agreement. Neither does it imply that members have capitulated. Instead, consensus is achieved when every team member can say, "I have had the opportunity to express my views fully, and they have been thoughtfully considered by the other members of the team. Even though this solution may not be the one I believe is optimal, I think it works, and I will support it."

While conflict resolution in groups differs somewhat from individuals resolving a disagreement, there are similarities between the two processes. The principles that apply to effective conflict resolution apply whether two or several people are involved in the negotiations.

Conflict can be either constructive or destructive. Much will be determined by how the disagreement is managed and by how the participants regard each other. Managed effectively, when the participants view each other with respect, resolving differences can actually help the team function more efficiently because discussing problems increases awareness, encourages change and increases motivation. If we don't know something is broken, we can't fix it. Often teams, like individuals, amble along until they are forced to reevaluate what has been causing the problem, and then, the members usually want to improve the situation.

Conflict can also serve to reduce small tensions among the team members. We are inclined to allow problems to escalate to the boiling point before we are motivated to deal with them. Clearing the air before the explosion occurs helps maintain good relationships. In fact, conflict resolution can enrich relationships when each person realizes that the relationship can withstand discord. Many times we are intimidated by conflict because we are afraid that it will cause a major breakdown in rapport. Once

Conflict resolution can enrich relationships when each person realizes that the relationship can withstand discord.

we learn that this isn't true, we become more confident about the stability of the alliances and about resolving future disagreements.

There are no guarantees when human behavior is involved, but generally speaking, approaching the controversy in a non-defense building, fair way will increase the likelihood that the dispute will be resolved favorably. Attacking the problem rather than the individuals, defining and narrowing the problem, expressing empathy, and making nonjudgmental statements are ways to reduce the likelihood that there will be bloodshed, an annoying end to any meeting. Conflict among team members comes from a host of different directions—some interpersonal and some cultural. Regardless of the source of the conflict, when left unchecked, conflict hampers the team's progress and damages interpersonal relationships.

Understanding team building means understanding how individual members' characteristics and personalities unite to form the unique culture of a given team. Satisfaction, performance, productivity, effectiveness, and turnover depend, to a large degree, on the socio-emotional make-up of the team. No two teams are alike. However, when we understand some of the universal factors that contribute to successful interactions, we can adapt and adjust our communication behavior to the situation and make choices that will benefit the team and us personally.

Strengthening the performance of a work team requires a clear understanding of each individual's role in working toward organizational goals and a strong appreciation of behavioral differences. Through candid, responsive communication, you can help build commitment, promote trust, and foster respect for the diverse talents of each team member.

COACH A WINNING TEAM

SUMMARY

*"Treat a person as he is, and he will remain as he is.
Treat a person as if he were what he could be and should be,
and he will become what he could be and should be."*

Under the direction of a competent leader, a successful team will evolve over time. The leader who sees into the future and anticipates the team's productivity can take steps to ensure that outcome.

Attracting, retaining, and developing top talent are the leader's primary challenges. Getting these same people to work together is the next. Sometimes that means they will work individually toward the organization's objectives. At other times, they will need to accomplish the more daunting task of working as a high performance team. The ability to inspire effective teamwork is often the linchpin in your long-term success as a boss, but it doesn't happen automatically. Rather, a constellation of factors determines whether a team will succeed in realizing its goals:

1. Evidence that you really need a team

2. Cohesive efforts

3. Goal accomplishment

4. Better meetings

5. Effective conflict resolution

The key parts of the team, the individuals, must join together in a way that harnesses the synergy of the team. A team is a living, dynamic, open system that interacts within itself and with the environment, and even though each team is unique, each shares a common principle: Whatever affects one part of the team affects all its parts and many other parts of the supra-system, your organization.

CHAPTER 9

DON'T HIRE SQUIRRELS
TO BE YOUR TOP DOGS

People aren't your most important assets. The <u>right</u> people are.
—JIM COLLINS, *GOOD TO GREAT*

Bad hiring decisions cost organizations, both in dollars and lost opportunities. But getting the right people in the right places doing the right thing is not easy. It requires painstaking efforts and objective information. Mergers, acquisitions, downsizing, and growth all require an unprecedented need for information about key executives and a framework for assessing the competencies required to lead people during extraordinary times. Accurately evaluating employees for hire and promotion involves more than guesswork and subjectivity. The formula is simple but not easy: hire well, develop talent, and plan succession.

"Russian Doll" management, the phenomenon by which managers repeatedly hire and promote miniature versions of themselves, will not take organizations where they need to go. Instead, ingenious solutions to tomorrow's complicated problems will demand diversity of thought and creativity. As Richard Florida, author of *The Flight of the Creative Class*, put it: "The United States may well have been the Goliath of the twentieth-century, but it will only take just half a dozen twenty-first-century Davids to wear it down." Finding the superlative leaders of tomorrow who will be able to help the U.S. stay a formidable force requires hiring the best and brightest people *now*. However, many organizations continue to hire squirrels instead.

WHAT IS A SQUIRREL?

Simply put, a squirrel is a creature that does not belong in your organization. It is a creature that, no matter how much you try, will for now and always be a squirrel. You can't fix squirrels. Trying to do so is a little like marrying a person that you hope you can change. It just doesn't happen. Squirrels are uncooperative, aggressive, destructive creatures that will cost your company significant sums of money. In fact, some researchers estimate that a squirrely hire can cost your company up to four times that person's yearly salary. For example, if you are hiring someone for a position that earns $100,000 a year, you are quickly facing the loss of almost half a million dollars of damage if that person doesn't work out.

> *If you are hiring someone for a $100,000 per year salary, you are quickly facing the loss of almost half a million dollars if that person doesn't work out.*

Even when the interviewer has years of experience and training, squirrels are not easy to spot, however. For instance, I met Jason in 2002. He was polished. He was handsome. He was articulate. He looked me right in the eye and gave me a firm, not crushing handshake. He flashed a pearly white smile that indicated many hours of laser whitening. He was *everything* I wanted him to be—for my client. He made such a strong first impression on me that I just knew he would do the same for my client's customers.

Before meeting Jason, I had taken a look at his assessment data, so I also knew he was bright, focused, success oriented, and good with people. He was all we could hope for. The only remaining step to his being hired was the interview. During it, I asked the usual questions, and Jason had a well-thought-out answer to each one. He was even able to say something meaningful when I asked, "What are some of your weaknesses?" Instead of the usual malarkey answer of "I'm too hard on myself and expect perfection all the time," he said that he had to work on giving more feedback and coaching to his direct report, something that every boss in the world needs to do.

We were almost finished when I said, "Tell me about your last performance review." Suddenly, Jason's eyes rolled back in his head, like Linda Blair in the *Exorcist*, his head spun around, and green slime spewed forth. In a demonic voice, he answered, "Well, keep in mind that my boss is a menopausal redneck!" Well, I'm no redneck, but few confuse me with a pubescent prom queen either. Although handsome and articulate, Jason is a squirrel.

About a year later I met John, an executive who exuded self-confidence. His confidence, in fact, bordered on arrogance. He knew that this was a slam dunk, and all he had to do was tolerate this annoying interview with me. He had been drinking a Diet Coke while he had been testing, so I invited him to bring it with him, as I usually do. This was not a usual circumstance, however.

Several questions into the interview I noticed that John was not drinking *from* the Diet Coke can; he was spitting *into* it. Throughout the hour-long interview, John answered questions and spit tobacco. Concentrating on my notes, I tried not to look, but like a car accident, he drew my gaze. I noticed each time he smiled, a speck of tobacco traveled from one tooth to another. I found myself speculating on the next destination of the speck instead of listening to John's responses. John is highly qualified and intelligent but nonetheless, a squirrel.

Let's contrast Jason and John with Tim, whom I met about the same time. Tim was a bright, dedicated, honest, and eager engineer. What he wasn't, was slick. He came to see me with a haircut that seemingly one of his children had given him; his shirt was half in and half out of his pants; his handshake was limp and just included only several of my fingers; his eyebrows looked like sea urchins on his forehead; and he avoided direct eye contact.

Clearly, organizations want to avoid hiring squirrels, but how can you tell a squirrel from a non-squirrel?

In general, Tim looked like an unmade bed. The only thing missing was a pocket protector for his slide rule and compass. Yet, there was something that told me that there was more to Tim than met the eye, thank goodness! When I gave him cognitive assessments, he blew the top off the range. All his personality data indicated that he was shy but determined to do whatever it takes to succeed.

As the interview progressed, Tim started to relax. He was quick to smile, genuine, and warm. In short, he had much to offer my client, but when I called to give them feedback, they were less than enthusiastic about him, pointing out that he was introverted and a little socially clumsy. I stuck to my guns and assured them that with some help, Tim could be a real asset to their company.

Now, a few years later, Tim is president of a division of this large organization, and Tim has proved he is most assuredly not a squirrel. Clearly, organizations want to avoid hiring squirrels, but how can you tell a squirrel from a non-squirrel?

START WITH A CLEAR JOB DESCRIPTION

The first step in the process of avoiding an unfortunate squirrel hire is to have a clear picture of the person you *do* want. Therefore, the hiring process needs to begin with a well-written description of the job function. In addition to giving you a specific picture of what you want, it will give prospective employees an understanding of what the job entails before the time and expense of the interviewing process begins.

A useful job description outlines the roles and responsibilities that anyone doing this job would need to assume. Then, it describes the scope of work, reporting relationships, and the minimum skills, education, and experience it will take to do that job well. The more specific these are, the easier time you will have deciding on the specific *competencies* a person will need to do this job well.

> *The more specific you are in the job description, the easier time you will have deciding on the specific competencies a person will need to do this job well.*

Prioritizing these competencies will then give you a framework for evaluating whether a candidate meets the company's needs. Sometimes a competency would be nice to have, but not critical. However, if you are distracted by a particular applicant's lack of a noncritical competency, a good person might take his or her talents to your competitor. Therefore, forcing yourself to evaluate the three to five *essential* skills or personality characteristics a solid candidate needs to possess will keep your focus keen. Another advantage of an effective job description is the description and delineation of competencies will imply the interview questions and strategies. (See Appendix D).

Once you streamline these procedures, the rest of the hiring process should run more smoothly, a critical aspect of moving quickly so that top candidates don't get away because you were too bogged down in mapping out a course of action. Even though this is a time-consuming method in the short run, and one that you'd rather see Human Resources handle, if you don't do your due diligence at this stage, you are very likely to end up with a squirrel on your payroll, possibly working for you.

SET THE SQUIRREL TRAP

Catching a squirrel is no easy task. It takes patience, knowledge, and experience. It also takes the ability to set a good squirrel trap. Ask any bird-watcher about squirrels, and you will get a dissertation about the frustrations of trapping the pesky rodent devils and keeping them away from bird feeders. Squirrels are wiry and wily. They can wiggle out of most situations and scamper off to destroy the property of some other unsuspecting chump.

Unlike their furry counterparts, however, the human version of squirrels, in some cases, has a large brain and well-developed strategies for subterfuge. Therefore, you will need to be equally prepared with your own tactics for trapping them. Catching them off guard, interviewing better, and collecting more

> Catching them off guard, interviewing better, and collecting more pertinent information are few of the steps you can take to set a squirrel trap.

pertinent information are a few of the steps you can take to set a squirrel trap. You'll have to devise your own combination of these, however, because if you use the traps made for the rodent types of squirrels, you'll definitely get a visit from those nice people at OSHA.

Put Them at Ease

The first step in setting the squirrel trap is to make the person feel comfortable. You will see people's true colors when they are relaxed. If the candidate is a squirrel, that fact is likely to surface if the person forgets to guard against it. Like Jason, the typical squirrel will be able to hoodwink you in the short run, but when concentration is compromised, you will get a glimpse of the real person (or squirrel) behind the façade.

One of the things I do before an interview is the same thing that most interviewers do. I take Maalox. That, and I look at the resumé. But in addition to looking for the usual things like experience and education, I search for something that we have in common. If the person has lived in a part of the world that I have, I make note of that; if we went to the same school, I notice that; if we have the same ex-husband, I remember that too. I look for any shared experience that we might have. Whatever the hook, I use it to make the person feel more comfortable. Then, before starting the questions, I refer to the thing we have in common, often by making a joke about it: "Well, it looks as if we were both able to escape Southern Illinois unscathed."

Joking and using appropriate humor are ways to encourage others to lower their guard. For instance, I usually start by offering candidates something to drink: "Coffee? Leaded or unleaded?" "Coke? Want rum with that?" "Some overpriced designer water that tastes exactly like tap water?" It's not hilarious stuff, but it does serve the purpose. It causes a smile or laugh, and the ice is broken. Once that happens, you'll be able to conduct an interview that unmasks even the most cunning squirrels.

Improve Interviewing

The second phase of trap setting is to interview smarter. There are volumes of books written on the subject of good interviewing techniques, but here are a few that you may not have considered:

- ❑ *Ask why they left their last job.* Most seasoned interviewers make this a part of their protocol. The words of the candidate's answer are not as critical as the nonverbal responses, however. The candidate will have rehearsed a good reason for leaving: The position was eliminated; opportunities for growth were minimized; a merger caused redundancy in positions. All of these are valid reasons for leaving, but you have to be sure the answer is true. Instead of looking at your notes or reading from a resumé, look at the person's eyes when you ask this one. Is the person looking you in the eye? Did the eyes dart left or right? Any facial touching? Fidgeting? Touching other objects? Crossing their fingers? All can be an indication that the person is not telling the truth.

- ❑ *Ask why they want to work in your organization.* This one will show whether they have done their homework. How is their energy and enthusiasm? If they are just looking for a job, that will show too.

- ❑ *Give hypothetical scenarios and ask what they would do in each.* No one can prepare for these kinds of questions, so you will get a glimpse of the thinking patterns of the individual. Most interviewers already do this one, but examining your scenarios and asking yourself whether they really get to the heart of what you're trying to discover can help you improve the value of the questions.

❑ *Ask about their areas for improvement*. Everyone asks this one, so applicants anticipate it and prepare the drivel responses. But you can push back and catch them off guard when they answer, "I expect too much from myself." By saying, "Oh, come on. Every applicant since the Pharaoh hired pyramid workers has used that one. Let me guess. You're also a perfectionist and work too much on weekends? What's a real one? What would your direct reports tell me? What would your boss tell me?" If, after some serious probing on your part, the person still can't come up with any areas for improvement, the person is either unconscious or seriously dedicated to impression management.

Improving interviewing is both an art and a science. Some people are just perceptive and insightful. That part can't be learned. But anyone can learn to be a more disciplined interviewer. If you ask the right questions, take copious notes, and follow a protocol, you'll improve as an interviewer. In general, follow the 80/20 rule. Talk about 20% of the time, and listen the other 80%.

Follow the 80/20 rule—talk about 20% of the time and listen the other 80%.

As the first page of this book mentioned, every leader needs to be honest, hardworking, and smart. If a job candidate isn't those things, no amount of coaching and development will help. Unfortunately, sometimes the lights are on, but there's just nobody in the office. If you want A players instead of C players, you will need to concentrate on developing a structured interview system that focuses on discovering whether or not an applicant possesses the critical characteristics for getting the job done.

Carefully worded behavioral interview questions can help you address intelligence, integrity, achievement drive, and additional areas that might be important for this person's success in your company. (See Appendix D, page 178.) But sometimes the interview isn't enough to give you a clear picture of what the person is capable of doing and what he or she is likely to do; you'll need more information.

Collect Better Data

Finally, the last step in setting a squirrel trap is to aggregate more and better information. Most interviewers rely on a pre-determined process to gather data. They request a resumé, conduct an interview, check references, and have meetings with other members of the organization to discuss impressions. However, all this is still not always enough. Sometimes you'll just have to tie applicants down and inject them with sodium pentothal.

The use of psychometrics, assessments that have been validated for hiring, is one way to improve your hiring practices. A well-chosen battery of tests, one that includes both intellectual measures and personality assessments, can increase the validity of your conclusions. This combination measures applicants' current intellectual resources and forecasts the kinds of decision making and problem solving they are likely to engage in. I advocate using at least two cognitive measures, one timed and one untimed, to determine whether deadlines and pressure will affect performance. Numerical testing should also be included if the position requires budget or financial decision making.

I recommend using at least four instruments that measure different aspects of work-related personality traits. Personality assessments offer crucial information because they indicate the candidate's achievement drive, ethics, and reliability—essentials for every job in every company. They also provide information about other kinds of personality characteristics that may help or hinder the person's ability to fit in and do the job. For example, people skills are essential for individuals applying for a sales position or a job in human resources. They are not so important for solo performers like accountants and engineers who will not have direct report responsibilities. Similarly, flexibility and adaptability are important traits for someone who works in a field that changes quickly and unexpectedly. They are not so critical for routine jobs that tend to stay the same most of the time.

All testing is not helpful, however. In fact, no testing is better than bad testing. Using only one assessment, using instruments that are not validated for use in making hiring decisions, and using tests that don't measure what you need not only waste time and money, but can put you at risk legally. Before you know it, you'll get to meet those lawyers who advertise on your local television channel, the ones who ask, "Have you been discriminated against in hiring?"

Finally, having someone who has been trained in interpreting psychometrics is essential. This is not something you can typically pick up in a six-week night course. Rather, the ability to aggregate the data from all the assessments is both a science and an art that requires years of experience to master. The money spent to hire a qualified person to interpret the data, usually less than a thousand dollars for most positions, is minimal when compared to the cost of a bad new hire.

The second way to gather more relevant information is to check references, again, a practice that most hiring professionals adhere to. However, armed with the information from the better interview and the assessment results, the decision maker can ask improved questions of the reference. For example, if the data indicate that the candidate doesn't respond well to unexpected changes, you might ask the reference, "In general, how does this person handle surprises?" "Routine tasks?" "Boredom?" The right answer won't be so apparent, so the person giving the reference is more likely to give an honest answer. Open "How?" "What?" questions can help too. You can ask what qualities the candidate is known for. How does he set priorities? How does she include others in decision making? Rather than responding with a simple yes or no, the reference might be encouraged to expound more on the particular characteristic in question, but not always.

In his book, *Hiring Smart!,* Pierre Mornell suggested an unusual but perfectly legal way to find out if the candidate is a squirrel:

> Call references at what you assume will be their
> lunchtime—you want to reach an assistant or voice mail. If
> it's voice mail, leave this simple message. If it's an assistant,
> be sure that he or she understands the last sentence of
> your message. You say 'John (or Jane) Jones is a candidate
> for (the position) in our company. Your name has been
> given as a reference. Please call me back if the candidate
> was outstanding.

Mornell said the results will be both immediate and revealing. "If the candidate is outstanding or excellent, I guarantee that 8 out of 10 people will respond quickly and want to help." If, on the other hand, you receive no call, their silence will speak volumes—sometimes.

A word of caution about Mornell's advice: Most companies that have a human resource department train managers to defer all reference calls to them. So, if you are calling a company that is likely to have this rule, you won't receive a call back, except from HR to verify that the person worked for them during certain periods of time.

I call them the "Stepford HR Departments" because they all answer exactly the same: "I can only tell you that Joe Bagadonuts worked here from June 1997 until March of 2005. That is all I can tell you." If you ask them another question, they will repeat, "I can only tell you...." (If you are an HR client of mine, by the way, continue to do this exactly).

However, when a specific person has been given as a reference, ask if you can call that person at home. That sometimes circumvents the HR rules. It doesn't work all the time, but sometimes you'll get lucky. Once you have all the salient data, you are ready to ask yourself the important question.

CAN YOU FIX A SQUIRREL?

There is an expression, "Never try to teach a pig to sing. It will frustrate you, and it will annoy the pig." In general, this is also sound advice when it comes to trying to fix a squirrel. But as we noticed in Tim's case, there are things that can be taught and learned, and with the right help, some candidates can become valuable contributors to your organization. However, knowing the difference between skills that can be developed and those that cannot is key.

Success orientation, intelligence, and integrity are essential traits of everyone in managment in any organization.

As mentioned previously, a success orientation, intelligence, and integrity are essential traits of everyone in management in any organization. They are also almost impossible to teach and learn. People can develop *behaviors* that indicate they possess these characteristics, but actually possessing them is another issue.

Similarly, decision-making skills, problem-solving abilities, learning rate, and creativity are also difficult to develop. People can improve in these areas, but the progress is slow and not usually significant enough to make a difference. By the time a person is applying for a job, especially an executive position, these talents will be resistant to change.

On the other hand, people skills, managerial skills, and presentation skills are easier to develop. With time and commitment, an individual can improve significantly in these areas. In fact, if a person has the ability to learn quickly, she or he will also be able to acquire new technical skills or industry knowledge fast enough to be an asset to the hiring organization. I have advised clients who want to find someone to fill a position to search for smart people who learn quickly, even if they don't have the industry experience that would be ideal.

A mistake that many companies make is weighing experience too much in the hiring process. In some areas it's critical; in others it would just be nice to have. If you're hiring a brain surgeon, you'll probably want someone who has taken a few medical classes and previously performed a few procedures. But is decision making and problem solving really all that different in your world? If you want someone

> *A mistake that many companies make is weighing experience too much in the hiring process.*

who has experience in making the same kinds of decisions you've always made, then you'll need to look for that, but when would that be a good idea? Chances are, you're looking for new ideas and fresh approaches, so don't be swayed too much by people who have 10 years of experience that is really just one year ten times.

For example, do you suppose that prior to 9/11 Rudy Giuliani had any experience with unexpected terrorist attacks on the World Trade Center Twin Towers? Of course not, but he did have practice with solving problems that had never existed before and was able to transfer that experience to a new situation. Following the devastation of Hurricane Katrina, many leaders drew criticism. When the local, state, and federal agencies all seemed to drop the ball, whom did they call? Coast Guard Vice Admiral Thad Allen, who had never had any experience helping a city like New Orleans recover from a Category Five storm.

Yet, drawing on his previous training and experience, he was able to take over and move things forward. He made decisions, solved unfamiliar problems, and learned quickly, three of the hallmarks of successful leaders. Allen had an oft-used saying that guided him in this crisis: "Transparency breeds self-correcting behavior." He created transparency by shining the light of media scrutiny on the entire recovery project, and let the American people judge their efforts for themselves.

Giuliani and Allen provide examples of the value of hiring people based on a proven track record of analytical reasoning and problem solving. Whatever the case or hiring scenario, even if a candidate has experience, education, and training, if that person is really a squirrel, in the long run, hiring that individual will be a decision that many will rue.

10 REASONS NOT TO HIRE SQUIRRELS

1. Not champions of innovation, squirrels are known as "living fossils." They haven't changed in 5 million years. What are the chances they will be able to handle expected, much less unexpected change in your company? And respond to shifting priorities? Won't happen.

2. Squirrels resolve conflict by foot stomping, tail flagging, chattering, and chasing. Not many people like conflict and even fewer are good at resolving it, but squirrely responses to conflict in your organization will get you another call from those nice lawyers who advertise on your local TV stations.

3. Aggressive and uncooperative, 32% of adult males have torn ears. Tear just one ear in corporate America, and you have huge problems and another pesky call.

4. Not good team players, squirrels are asocial and solitary. If the job requires any kind of collaboration, teamwork, or coordination of effort, a squirrel is not your rodent of choice.

5. When confronted with a threat, squirrels stand motionless, swallow hard, and chew fast—so much for overcoming obstacles. Most companies require more of a "can do" spirit that squirrels just don't seem to be able to embody.

6. The brains of squirrels are seldom engaged. The stomach rules. Some part of the brain has to work for success in most companies. The stomach should play a much lesser role.

7. Because their sweat glands are in their paws, squirrels are lousy handshakers. Will this help build rapport with clients?

8. There are 1600 different species of squirrels, but they are all seed-stealing thieves. Squirrels are sometimes tough to classify by the specific genus, but they all share the characteristic of being thieves. There's no place for an employee who will have a paw in the till.

9. Squirrels spend most of their day sleeping and are usually only active around lunchtime.

10. Although cute and furry, squirrels are gnawing beasts that destroy property and make no attempts at restitution.

Bringing squirrels into the organization compromises the leadership pipeline that each company needs to fuel. However, a crisis often causes a company to make a poor hiring decision that costs them dearly. An alternative is to hire temporary help until a high potential candidate becomes available.

Hiring smart is the first step to making sure the organization has the right people coming into the organization, but it is only the first step. Developing talented individuals for progression and succession is critical for the growth and success of the company over the long term.

DEVELOP HIGH-POTENTIAL CANDIDATES

One of the surest ways to attract the best and brightest in your industry is to develop the reputation for developing your people. A players want and need to flourish, so they will go where they see the most opportunity to be on a winning team. There are a few things that most A Players want from their companies:

❏ A high-performance culture

❏ The excitement of working with other A players

❏ The opportunity to grow

❏ Competitive pay and stock options

However, in general, the best way to keep A players comes from bosses regularly asking their direct reports what they want to do to stretch performance. This professional "stretching" can come in several forms: internal coaching, external training, education, and technical training.

> *When they have talent, they are faced with the new task of making sure their stars are not lured away from them with one of the many calls their project leaders receive from head - hunters.*

The construction industry has recently become both blessed and plagued with competition for top talent. On the positive side, successful companies are growing quickly; on the negative side, the leaders of these companies are experiencing a war for talent. When they realize they have talent, they are faced with the new task of making sure that their stars are not lured away from them with one of the many calls their project leaders receive from headhunters.

Jeff Bogart, General Manager of Vantage Homes, St. Louis, received the help he needed for "stretching to be a better leader." He found that participating in executive evaluations and 360 feedback helped him better understand how his actions affected his team. Bogart reported that coaching helped him clarify his goals, focus on solutions to people problems, and grow his business.

By using an external coach, Bogart began to realize the importance of his role as internal coach for his own direct reports. One way to start the process and to build trust between the boss and direct reports is through two-way conversations. However, bosses sometimes focus on *giving* rather than *receiving* feedback. Bogart reversed this order by engaging in a direct report meeting that was based on their 360, multi-rater feedback results. He reported that he found the experience both eye-opening and beneficial. Once he knew how his behavior affected his team's productivity, he was equipped to make changes and to offer more coaching himself.

One of the reasons these critical two-way discussions are not occurring in more organizations is bosses feel uncomfortable, unprepared, or ineffective in such encounters. They avoid the very conversations that could help them build better relationships and increase productivity among the people who need their direction and support.

Jan Kraemer, Vice President of Human Resources for McCarthy Building Companies, came to these conclusions several years ago when she realized that people in the construction world receive a great deal of training and education about technical issues but very little about leading others. To correct this problem and to further McCarthy's efforts to be a "talent magnet," she and other leaders at McCarthy implemented a performance appraisal system so that bosses can learn how to coach direct reports, a training program to teach leadership skills, and a mentoring program to anchor the lessons in real world examples. The appraisal system has been in effect since 2003; two classes of high potentials have completed leadership training; and one group has completed a year of formal mentoring. The feedback from participants has been encouraging.

However, Kraemer is quick to note that one-time training is not the answer. Rather, ongoing training efforts and continued mentoring programs are likely to help McCarthy remain an employer of choice in an industry that competes for top talent. In their follow-up evaluations of the training sessions, participants reported that they now better understand how their behavior affects others and the steps they can take to secure their places as future leaders at McCarthy.

As Jan Kraemer knows, if McCarthy invests in their talent, "by the time they are needed at higher levels, they are much better equipped to handle the people side of leadership." She also realizes that the return on investment is not always immediately apparent, but the quick promotions and low turnover at McCarthy imply that what they're doing is working, so they are better equipped to plan the success of their company. In short, companies like McCarthy work to hire and develop bosses that no one wants to leave.

DON'T HIRE SQUIRRELS TO BE YOUR TOP DOGS

SUMMARY

Smart companies, ones that want to select and retain talent in industries that are characterized by pirating and stiff competition, know that they must pioneer new ways to keep squirrels from becoming their top dogs. Instead of engaging in their current practices, they need to hire smarter.

What can companies do to make better hiring decisions?

1. Know who you're looking for and don't settle for anything less.
2. Improve interviewing.
3. Collect better data.

Identifying an individual's strengths and approaches to work *before* making hiring decisions will help enhance reliability and build confidence that your company is hiring the most qualified candidate. Once this step is complete, the individual's boss can map out a plan and timeline for developing skills and gaining experience that will enable the person to move forward in the organization, all important aspects of planning for the organization's succession and success.

We know that top performers want to work with other high-potential people; therefore, one of the best ways to attract and retain the stars your industry has to offer is to build a high-performance culture and provide opportunities for growth. When this happens, you won't have to worry about recruiters calling your people. They'll be *your* top dogs, and they will want to stay with you, largely because you provide the opportunity to work with others who are committed to excellence.

CHAPTER 10

BE THE BOSS THEY WON'T WANT TO LEAVE

Leadership is lifting a person's vision to higher sights,
the raising of a person's performance to a higher standard,
the building of a personality beyond its normal limitations.
—PETER DRUCKER

Ladies and gentlemen, the captain has turned on the seat belt sign. Please return to your seats and make sure your seat belt is fastened tightly around you. We will be encountering some unexpected turbulence.

I have no idea what that turbulence will be, the source of it, the cause of it, or the cure for it. But I can guarantee it will come. And like the captain of a 747, your job as the boss will be to make decisions that help all those on board with you navigate the sometimes unfriendly and uncharted skies of your particular industry and organization. You will make decisions that affect you, but more importantly, you will make decisions that will affect many, possibly thousands of other people. That's what bosses do. They take charge in turbulent time.

Why would anyone want to be led by you? That's the question that needs to frame your journey to better leadership. If you have a hard time answering that one, try this one, "Would you want you for a boss?" I often ask this of my clients. When I meet with an awkward silence, a stare like a dog watching a ceiling fan, or fidgeting, I infer that the answer is "no." The next questions are, "What makes you think others want you for their boss?" and "What are you doing that you wouldn't want your boss to do?" As simple as the exercise is, it is eye opening in almost every case.

To truly be the magnetic boss, you'll need to rouse others with confidence in you and inspire them with assurance in themselves. Lou Holtz, famed Notre Dame football coach, captured the essence of this daunting task in three questions people always ask about their leaders:

1. Are you committed to excellence?
2. Can I trust you?
3. Do you care about me?

There are many myths about great leadership and just as many pieces of advice to match them. But Lou Holtz's questions make it all very simple. Can your direct reports answer "yes" to all three? A good way to begin to answer the question is to understand what leadership *isn't*.

DISPEL THE MYTHS

Even though people have been talking and writing about leadership for centuries, we continue our obsession with understanding it. There have been inspirational religious leaders, transformational wartime leaders, charismatic leaders—some good, others horrendous, and still others as ordinary as Little League coaches. They don't seem to share too many circumstances or characteristics that would justify the formulation of an irrefutable explanation.

Yet, they all have one thing in common: others followed. The purpose of this discussion is not to argue for or against any one theory but to offer some observations based on my more than 25 years of consulting and thousands of hours of coaching. Here are four things that just don't seem to be true.

Charisma is Essential

Charisma is great if you can muster it, but quite frankly, most people most of the time can't. Many companies choose technical or business experts to be their leaders, people who are knowledgeable and dedicated, but not necessarily magnetic. Their appeal is their authenticity, not their charm.

In conducting research for his best seller, *Good to Great*, Jim Collins and his team wanted to know whether there are companies that defy gravity and convert long-term mediocrity, or worse, into long-term superiority. And if there are, what are the universal distinguishing characteristics that cause a company to go from good to great?

Using tough benchmarks, Collins and his team identified a set of elite companies that had made the leap to great results and sustained those results for at least fifteen years. Among the surprising conclusions, the researchers were shocked to discover the type of leadership required to turn a good company into a great one:

Compared to high-profile leaders with big personalities who make headlines and become celebrities, the good-to-great leaders seem to have come from Mars. Self-effacing, quiet, reserved, even shy—these leaders are a paradoxical blend of personal humility and professional will. They are more like Lincoln and Socrates than Patton or Caesar.

These "Level 5" leaders, as Collins calls them, channel their ego needs away from themselves and into the larger goal of building a great company. They are incredibly ambitious, but their ambition is first for the institution, not themselves. They are fanatically driven and infected with an incurable need to produce stellar results, yet they demonstrate a compelling modesty. They look out the window to apportion credit and in the mirror to assign blame.

All leaders have one thing in common: others followed.

People are motivated to work for modest, focused leaders because they trust them and their decision making. Introverted, shy engineers who work tenaciously to overcome their preference for isolated work should be heartened that they don't necessarily have to exude personality to draw others to work for them. They often need to concentrate on changing other behaviors, but they can put this one aside.

Leadership theorist, Warren Bennis, suggested,

> Good leaders make people feel that they're at the very heart of things, not at the periphery. Everyone feels that he or she makes a difference to the success of the organization. When that happens, people feel centered and that gives their work meaning.

Not every great leader has the capacity to be charismatic, but as Collins and Bennis pointed out, each boss certainly possesses what it takes to make people feel that they are essential to the working of the company. When they feel that, how likely is it that they will leave?

The Boss Has to Know Everything

Another myth that causes unwarranted angst among many bosses is the perception that they have to know everything. Certainly the more business knowledge and technical expertise you bring to the table, the better, but knowing everyone else's job is not critical, and it's not realistic.

During the beginning of the war in Iraq, Air Force General Richard Myers was the Chairmen of the Joint Chiefs of Staff. He was the ultimate voice for all branches of the military, the person who had to influence policy and procedure that affected thousands of military personnel throughout the world. His authority and power held sway with politicians, soldiers, and sailors, yet I doubt he could change the tire of an F-18 fighter jet. To think that he would spend his time trying to learn to do so or that he would even be concerned about how it is done is ludicrous. The crew chief who had this knowledge would be many, many steps down the chain of command from General Myers.

Imagining that a four-star general would concern himself with tire changing is only slightly more ridiculous than thinking that you should know everything that everyone under you does. You don't have to. You just need to understand the chain of command and know who the "go to" person is for information. If bosses clutter their minds with information that others have, they are being redundant. One of the people in the equation is not necessary. The question you need to continue to ask yourself is, "Is this the best use of my time and energy?"

Bosses don't have to know everything, and they don't have to have all the answers either. No one can have all the answers, and no one expects you to have all of them. However, you are expected to recruit and retain people at all levels of your organization who *do* have the answers. Ultimately, you will be known by the contributions that these people make to the overall company objectives. *Their* achievements will be *your* results and the measure of *your* excellence. If you are smart enough to hire and develop people who are smarter and more talented than you are, you will be known as a daring and bold leader who left a legacy of excellence.

The Boss Has to Do More Than Anyone Else

Bosses have the duty to model excellence and to expect it from their direct reports. However, they are not paid to actually do the work. This is a tricky part of the transition from solo performer to boss. The job of the leader is to make decisions, solve problems and coach *others* so *they* can actually touch the work. As you move up the chain of command, your responsibilities to the company are less and less about the amount of work you actually do and more and more about what you influence others to do.

The problem is that this mindset robs the boss of the euphoric feelings of accomplishment that drove his or her success to this point. Chances are you're the boss because you love the feelings of completion and attainment. You've always loved the feeling you've enjoyed from a job well done. Now others have those feelings, and you're on the sidelines. Taking on leadership responsibilities means adjusting attitudes and beliefs to reflect the new world in which you are often not the doer of the most interesting, challenging, or fun work.

> *Your primary task is to develop the bench. Who is your replacement?*

Leaders Are Great Coaches

They really aren't, but they should be. Data from thousands of multi-rater feedback instruments indicate that most bosses are not even adequate coaches. In fact, most bosses see coaching as an activity that is nice to engage in if there's time left over after everything else is finished. You might be the most charismatic, inspirational visionary, but if you don't take the time to develop your people, they will be denied one of the primary reasons to stay with you. After all, the final test of great leaders is that they left behind women and men who are willing to carry on after them.

In addition to making decisions and solving problems, your primary task is to develop the bench. Who is your replacement? Would that person know what to do if you were hit by a bus this evening? If not, you have compromised the future of your organization by not preparing someone to do what you do. No matter how indispensable you would like to think you are to the company, part of your job is to make sure you aren't. That means you need to have a plan for developing the skills and knowledge in one or more people to take over if you can no longer perform your duties. Part of that process begins by creating a reality in which people can answer "yes" to each of Lou Holtz's questions.

COMMIT TO EXCELLENCE

People want to play on a winning team, and most realize that hard work and sacrifice make a team win. Football players suit up to practice in the 100-degree temperatures of August, not because they like it, but because they know it is part of attaining excellence. Your direct reports are no different. They expect you to demand what it takes to separate your company from the competition.

During his tenure on the speaking circuit, Lou Holtz told stories of inspiring his team by saying that he had called the coach at the University of Michigan, Bo Schembechler, to see if he would agree to easy practices for his players so that the Notre Dame players could take it easy too. As Holtz told his team, Bo said he wouldn't agree, so he couldn't let them off easy either. As he explained, if the competition is doing it, we have to do it if we are going to beat them in the opening game of the season.

> *People want to play on a winning team and most realize that hard work and sacrifice make a team win. Your direct reports expect you to demand of them what it takes to separate your company from the competition.*

Like Holtz's players, from the time we are children, we understand that excellence requires hard work. People won't grouse about it if they think you are really striving for superiority.

What is the essence of excellence? Excellent bosses are all alike in that they commit to their own improvement, an ongoing and never ending quest to attain new levels of distinction. Inferior bosses are often second-rate in their own ways, but excellence is defined by universal traits.

The single worst thing that can happen to cause you to cease being excellent is that you will exhaust your intellectual capital and reach your level of incompetence. Early in your career you dedicated yourself to learning, growing, and experiencing. Now, you are bogged down in the perpetual challenges of getting results. Most of us have heard the story of the successful wood cutter taking time to sharpen his saw and the unsuccessful one toiling day after day because he didn't think he could take time to sharpen his. Trying to cut with a dull saw keeps you in motion and lets others know you are busy and dedicated, but it's not the smartest way to operate. You are so busy *doing* that you forget about learning, the intellectual equivalent to sharpening the saw. You need to learn faster now, so take the time to learn how to learn. It can pay enormous dividends.

Shortly after taking the helm of Tyson Foods, John Tyson realized that he wanted leadership development to pay enormous dividends in both the metaphorical and literal senses. Despite its size after the 2001 merger with International Beef Products, which brought its market cap to approximately $25 billion and its ranking well into the *Fortune* 100,

Tyson Foods was investing very little in developing leadership for the merged organization. Tyson decided to change that. In 2002 John Tyson, his direct reports, and a group of external succession-planning experts began to change the ways the company chose and developed leaders. I was a member of the external team of succession planning experts, and here's what we did.

Working together, we mapped out an integrated succession plan that included leadership development for each of the people in key positions. The process began with an assessment that provided an in-depth look at each person's cognitive abilities, problem solving skills, leadership knowledge, and business related personality characteristics. Based on the assessment results and their multi-rater data, each participant received face-to-face feedback and

> *Gather relevant information about yourself. You probably already know most of your strengths and weaknesses, but knowing others' perceptions can be truly eye opening.*

coaching. Then, participants engaged in two follow-up coaching sessions and a leadership retreat during which the participants addressed actual business challenges, reflected on their personal leadership styles, and broadened their spheres of influence by meeting other high-potentials within the company.

During this entire process John Tyson challenged members of his executive team to make sure that promising leaders would be well versed in all aspects of the company's business and put the accountability for succession planning squarely on their shoulders. As Tyson pointed out, leaders "couldn't waffle about contributing their time and effort to the new talent development system; they couldn't 'protect' talent, hoard resources, or declare themselves immune from succession planning."

John Tyson's goal was and is to ensure that the company develops talent so leaders can execute current strategies while preparing to take on more complex roles. He wants to make sure that rising stars are challenged to achieve long-term success at Tyson and that senior leaders work to devise paths that consider multiple career possibilities for each high-potential candidate. Obviously, John Tyson is taking bold steps to ensure that he has bosses and a company no one wants to leave.

Drawing from Tyson's lessons, what can you do to develop your leadership path? The first step is to gather relevant information about yourself. You probably already know most of your strengths and weaknesses, but knowing others' perceptions can be truly eye opening. One of the best ways to find out is to ask. That can take several forms, but probably one of the most effective is the multi-rater 360 instrument, one of the components in Tyson's development process. A well-crafted survey will capture the opinions of direct reports, peers, and your boss, if you have one. Once you understand what their observations are, you will be able to take steps to improve in ways that they think you should.

Some interesting things happen when executives use 360 data for their own improvement. For example, Dennis Shriver, General Manager of Vantage Homes, Kansas City, is a boss who is dedicated to excellence. The leaders at Vantage quickly identified Shriver as a high-potential candidate and took the steps to make sure he moved quickly through the leadership pipeline. He attended skills-based leadership training, engaged in an executive development initiative, and received ongoing coaching from me, an external coach. Shriver pointed out that the coaching allowed it all to come together. Through regularly scheduled meetings with me, he began to be accountable for and focused on what needed to be done. He was not only made more aware of his strengths and weaknesses, he was also able to discuss how to improve himself in real life situations. Shriver understood the value of sharpening a saw, which is a good thing since he's in construction.

One way to start the process for building trust between the boss and direct reports is through two-way conversations.

Another factor that is related to excellence is a commitment to building trust. One way to start the process for building trust between the boss and direct reports is through two-way conversations. However, bosses sometimes focus too much on *giving* rather than *receiving* feedback. Shriver reversed this order by engaging in a direct report meeting that was based on their 360, multi-rater feedback results. He reported that he found the experience both eye-opening and beneficial. Once he knew how his behavior affected his team's productivity, he was equipped to make changes and to offer more coaching, all important first steps for answering the other questions most direct reports ask: "Can I trust you?" and " Do you care about me?"

FOSTER TRUST AND BUILD RAPPORT

Once your direct reports are sure that you are committed to personal and organizational excellence, they will want to know if they can trust you. Chapter One discussed the different kinds of trust in a general sense, but this particular question is personal. "Can I, your direct report, whose future, job satisfaction, and livelihood depend on your good judgment, trust you?" The answer needs to be, "Yes. You can trust me to be open when I can be, to be honest and ethical all the time, to be predictable when I can be, and to admit my mistakes." Nobody is perfect, and nobody gets it right the first time or every time after that. Your direct reports know you aren't perfect, they just don't tell you that they know.

When you try to cover your mistakes, pretend they didn't happen, or worse yet, blame them on someone else, you can forget about sustaining, much less building trust for a long, long time. Winston Churchill said it best: "Success is the ability to go from failure to failure without losing your enthusiasm." Churchill is a name that lives on because of his successes, but those who know history understand that he was not without his fiascoes or his critics. You won't be either; it's just one of those nasty realities of being in charge. Your direct reports will forgive your mistakes as long as they know you are committed to excellence, they can trust you, and they know you care.

An underrepresented concept is the boss's role as cheerleader, the person who strives to rally enthusiasm and energy so the team can play on, even when encountering a tougher team in a dirty fight.

The word "coach" is used throughout leadership books, and indeed has been used throughout this discussion. There's little argument that a great boss also needs to be a great coach. But an underrepresented concept is the boss's role as cheerleader, the person who strives to rally enthusiasm and energy so the team can play on, even when encountering a tougher team in a dirty fight. Observe the coaches on the sidelines of a Final Four game or a high-stakes playoff of any kind. Is there much difference between them and the cheerleaders? The cheerleaders jump more and wear cuter clothes, but they are fundamentally doing the same thing. Like an animated cheerleader, your job is to be the Energizer Bunny for your direct reports. It's your duty to be the power source that others know they can rely on. What if you don't feel energetic? Fake it.

For example, during my research on the Vietnam POW's, I met Gary, who had been an Air Force captain at the time of his capture. Even though he was a young man, he was the senior ranking officer in his unit. Gary and his team were captured in Laos, before there was any admission that the United States was operating in that country. Deep in his heart, Gary believed they would never come home alive. Yet, day after day, he communicated his optimism. He didn't feel it, but he forced himself to act as though he did. Soon, he learned that he felt better and that those under him in the chain of command remained heartened too. He gave his men hope, an intangible gift that sends a clear message of caring.

> Hope has two dimensions: willpower, or the desire to have a positive outcome, and waypower, the willingness to do what it takes to make constructive things occur.

In Gary's case, his optimism and energy literally played a role in those men surviving their captivity and returning home at the end of the war. Your role might not be a life-or-death situation, but it's one you will need to take seriously if others are to believe that you truly care about them. Helping them remain hopeful is a powerful way to send them that message.

For so many decades organizational research has been dominated by a desire to understand and ameliorate human dysfunction and problems in the workplace. The emphasis was on motivating disgruntled employees, improving dysfunctional attitudes, overcoming resistance to change, and coping with stress and burnout. Positive emotions, such as hope, were largely ignored. Hope is an attribute that hasn't traditionally been associated with leadership, but with recent work on the subject, new ways of understanding it are receiving attention.

To better understand its role, researchers engaged a large fast-food franchise chain. Fifty-nine managers of those restaurants participated in a study to measure whether hope affected leadership effectiveness. The simple answer is it does. The results indicated that "high hope" leaders had significantly better financial performance, subordinate retention, and satisfaction scores than the "low hope" participants.

According to these researchers, hope has two dimensions: *willpower*, or the desire to have a positive outcome, and *waypower*, the willingness to do what it takes to make constructive things occur. High hope individuals tend to be more certain about their goals and challenged by them. They value progress toward objectives as well as the objectives themselves. They enjoy interacting with others and readily adapt to new and collaborative relationships; they are less anxious in stressful situations, and they are more adaptive to environmental changes.

Instilling hope in your direct reports is one of the single most important gifts you can give them; it doesn't cost a thing; and anyone can give it at any time in any set of circumstances. Here are some suggestions:

❑ Communicate your own faith in them so they can develop their own "can do" attitude.

❑ Facilitate willpower by using participative decision making and empowering others to set specific stretch goals.

❑ Assist them in developing waypower by requiring well-developed action plans and contingency plans for achieving goals.

❑ Act as a sounding board for their thoughts, but instead of shooting holes in their ideas, guide them to their own conclusions by asking open-ended questions that encourage them to analyze more fully the implications of their decisions.

As I mentioned earlier, accomplishing some objectives can seem a little like trying to eat an elephant. The task is huge, and the feelings of accomplishment much removed from current efforts to complete it. Therefore, your direct reports may need for you to break down complex, long-term projects into smaller tasks with a deadline for each "bite" along the way. Accomplishing each step then builds hope that the next step and the one after that will also be attainable, with the ultimate realization of the objective becoming more realistic with each achievement.

Showing that you care about your direct reports through hope taps a type of positive thinking and action in people that is significantly related to important workplace outcomes. Stimulating the desire to achieve objectives, willpower and facilitating the discovery of paths to achieving the goals, waypower, leads to positive personal and performance outcomes.

BE THE BOSS THEY WON'T WANT TO LEAVE

SUMMARY

Understanding leadership better, committing to excellence, and letting others know they can trust you and you care about them are essential first steps to becoming the boss no one wants to leave. Yet, chances are, no matter how hard you try, you won't be a leader who will be remembered in the history books.

Your name won't be uttered in the same breath as Churchill, Gandhi, Eisenhower, or even Lou Holtz. People won't write books decades from now and include your quotes, neither will most remember you at all. That only happens to a handful of people who are blessed or cursed with circumstances and characteristics that coalesce in the right combinations during the exact times they are needed, with too many moving parts and variables to control.

However, each person has the capacity to improve. A company's success is ultimately a matter of people, yet managing employees for superior performance remains more an art than a science, and most bosses don't understand either. While most companies see the need for excellence in this arena, they are at a loss for systematic ways to bridge the gap between their level of capability and a higher one that leads to greater business value. But you now have the tools:

1. The F^2 Model of Leadership
2. The GLAD Communication Method
3. A visible, virtual and verbal communication technique
4. A coaching strategy to produce high scorers
5. The GLAD Performance Review model
6. Maintaining altitude, air speed, and ideas
7. Taking charge of change
8. A coaching system for winning teams
9. A hiring approach for attracting top dogs

Perhaps you don't have discretionary power to allocate large sums of money to developing all the ideas that you have read here, but you do have governance over your own behaviors.

You can begin with one or two goals that will make small but important moves in the right direction. For instance, you can commit to better listening; you can pledge to others that you will increase the number of performance management conversations you have throughout the year; you can promise to hold better meetings; you can give your word that you will take steps to know your direct reports better so that you understand their strengths and can help to build their hope for the future.

Not one of these costs money, yet any one will help you take important steps toward being the boss that no one wants to leave. So, put on your own oxygen mask first and become the boss they don't want to leave.

To laugh often and much; to win the respect of intelligent people and the affection of children; to earn the appreciation of honest critics and endure the betrayal of false friends; to appreciate beauty, to find the best in others; to leave the world a little better; whether by a healthy child, a garden patch or a redeemed social condition; to know even one life has breathed easier because you have lived. This is to have succeeded.

—RALPH WALDO EMERSON

GLAD COMMUNICATION PLANNING GUIDE

(G)et to the core of the performance issues.

❑ Put the problem in one sentence. The problem is: _____

_____

❑ Clearly identify the purpose of the discussion.

_____

❑ Use clear, concrete language.

(L)isten to the other first.

❑ Listen first.

❑ Don't interrupt.

❑ Summarize and paraphrase.

❑ Ask at least two open-ended questions. Open questions you'll ask:

1. _____

_____

2. _____

_____

(A)dd your own ideas.

❑ Comment on other's ideas first.

❑ Offer new or different ideas.

❑ From your point of view, explain exactly what needs to happen to solve this problem.

_____

_____

❑ Explain *why* this is important.

_____

(D)evelop an action plan.

❑ Identify two priorities that you think you will need to address.

1. _____

2. _____

❑ Break large projects into smaller parts with a deadline for each. (This will happen after the conversation.)

❑ Set approximate start and completion dates for each part. (If you can, leave these open, but if they are firm, identify them.)

❑ Schedule Follow up discussion and next steps.

RESOLVING CONFLICT

❑ What do you consider to be the main barriers to objective and constructive candor?

_____

❑ How can these barriers be eliminated or lowered?

_____

❑ What other problems must be resolved before you begin to tackle this problem?

_____

❑ Describe the overall nature of your present on-the-job relationship with the other person.

_____

❑ How would you describe what an ideal working relationship would be?

_____

❑ What have you done to cause the current conflict?

_____

❑ What resolution have you attempted?

_____

❑ What has the other person done to contribute to the current conflict?

_____

❑ What attempts has he or she made at resolution?

_____

❑ What major obstacles stand in the way of making this relationship ideal?

    What obstacles do you introduce?

    _____

    What obstacles does the other person introduce?

    _____

❑ What can be done to eliminate these barriers?

_____

❑ What other factors or people inhibit the relationship being ideal?

_____

❑ What benefits would accrue if the relationship were improved?

    Benefits to you?_____

    Benefits to the other person?_____

    Benefits to the organization? _____

❑ What adverse consequences to you, the other person and the organization might ensue if the relationship is not improved?

_____

❑ What can be done to improve the relationship so that the benefits are realized and the adverse consequences averted?

    What can you do?_____

    What can the other person do?_____

    What can others do? _____

JOB DESCRIPTION FORM

❑ Why does this job exist?

In two or three sentences encapsulate this person's role in the company.

_____

_____

_____

_____

_____

❑ To whom does this person report?

_____

❑ How many people will report to this person? _____

❑ What are their titles and responsibilities?

_____

_____

_____

_____

_____

_____

_____

❏ What are this person's responsibilities on a:

Daily basis:

_____

_____

_____

_____

Weekly basis:

_____

_____

_____

_____

Monthly basis:

_____

_____

_____

_____

Quarterly basis:

_____

_____

_____

_____

Yearly basis:

_____

_____

_____

_____

Please be as specific and detailed as possible. These responsibilities include both internal responsibilities and external responsibilities (what this person does for clients). Enumerate the responsibilities under each time frame with bullet points.

❑ What are the specific skills needed to perform this job?

_____

_____

❑ What specific knowledge is needed to perform this job?

_____

_____

❑ What experience is required?

_____

❑ What are the key success indicators in this job?

_____

_____

❑ Please indicate in rank order the Top Five characteristics that are most desirable for effective performance in this job:

___Written communication skills	___Adaptability to change
___Interpersonal skills	___Ability to work independently
___Ease with numbers	___Creation of good first impression
___Sales ability	___Tenacity & persistence
___Managerial ability	___Competitive drive
___Analytical reasoning skills	___Self-discipline
___Organizing and planning	___Willingness to accept supervision
___Reliability and dependability	___Customer focus
___Energy	___Assertiveness

SAMPLE INTERVIEW QUESTIONS

Capacity to Learn:

❑ Describe a situation in which you had to acquire a great deal of information quickly. How did you go about learning, and how successful were the outcomes?

❑ What kinds of things have you done since receiving your degree to continue your learning?

❑ In the past year, what specifically have you done to remain knowledgeable about the competitive environment, market, and trade dynamics as they relate to your job?

Integrity:

❑ Describe a situation in which the pressures to compromise your integrity were the strongest you have ever felt. What did you do?

❑ What is one of the most unpopular stands you have ever taken?

❑ When have you confronted unethical behavior or chosen not to say anything in order not to rock the boat?

❑ Under what circumstances have you found it justifiable to break a confidence?

Bias for Action:

❑ Have you significantly "raised the bar" for yourself or others? Explain how you did it, the problems encountered, the outcomes.

❑ What obstacles have you faced in your current job and what did you do to overcome them?

❑ When do you finally take "no" for an answer?

❑ What motivates you?

Global Perspective and Critical Thinking:

❑ What has been your experience in establishing operational plans?

❑ Tell me about a time when you helped to define vision and strategic direction for your current or previous organization.

❑ What has been your experience in making decisions and taking action when you had limited information?

❑ What is the best and worst mistake you've made in the last year?

❑ Would people describe you as more detail oriented or broad brush?

❑ What maxims do you live by?

Self-awareness:

❑ Have you received any sort of systematic or regular feedback from direct reports, clients, peers, supervisors? What did you learn?

❑ Describe a situation in which you were the angriest you have been in years.

Coaching Others and Building Strength:

❑ Tell me about a situation when you helped someone in career development. Describe the developmental objective and how you helped build a new skill set or over come deficiency to help advance the person's career. What was the process and outcome?

❑ How would your direct reports describe your approaches to training and developing them?

❑ What kinds of things have you done to stretch and challenge them to take on more responsibility.

Valuing Diversity:

❑ When have you actively confronted indications of discrimination or prejudicial behavior? What did you do?

❑ Describe a situation when you needed to serve as a role model to others about the importance of valuing diversity. What happened?

❑ Can you give me an example of a time that you were able to draw out a person's unique talents and their applicability to the organization?

People Skills:

❑ Tell me about a situation when you were expected to work with a person you disliked. What did you do?

❑ How would you describe your sense of humor?

❑ When there is a difference of opinion, how do you tend to handle the situation?

❑ Could you give me a couple of recent examples, one that had a favorable outcome and one that had an unfavorable one, of when you felt you needed to be highly assertive.

Chapter 1

Allen, L.A. (1958). *Management & Organizations.* New York: McGraw-Hill.

Allport, G.W. (1937). *Personality: A Psychological Interpretation.* New York: Holt.

Blake, R.R. & Mouton, J. S. (1985). *The Managerial Grid III: The Key to Leadership Excellence.* Houston: Gulf Publishing.

Branham, L. (2005). *The 7 Hidden Reasons Employees Leave: How to Recognize the Subtle Signs and Act Before It's Too Late.* American Management Association.

Cathcart, R.S. & Samovar, L.A. (1984). *Small Group Communication: A Reader.* Madison, WI: Wm. C. Brown Publishing.

Fiedler, F.E. (1967). *A Theory of Leadership Effectiveness.* New York: McGraw-Hill.

Galford, R. & Drapeau, A. (2003). *The Trusted Leader.* Free Press.

Hall, C.S. & Lindzey, G. (1957). *Theories of Personality.* New York: John Wiley & Sons Inc.

Hersey, P. & Blanchard, K. (1972). Situational Leadership. *Center for Leadership Studies.*

Howard, A. & Wilson, J. (Summer, 1982). *Leadership in a Declining Work Ethic.* California Management Review. 33-46.

Hodgetts, R. (1992). *Modern Human Relations at Work.* Fort Worth: Dryden Press.

Levitt, T. (Summer, 1976). The Management and The Post Industrial Society. *The Public Interest.*

Lewin, K., Lippitt, R. & White, R.K. (1939). Patterns of Aggressive Behavior in Experimentally Created Social Climates. *Journal of Social Psychology, 10,* 271-299.

Maslow, A.H. (1968). *Toward a Psychology of Being.* New York: D. Van Nostrand Co.

McGregor, D. (1960). *The Human Side of Enterprise.* New York: McGraw-Hill.

Munson, E. L. (1921). *The Management of Men.* New York: Holt.

Ryckman, R. (1985). *Theories of Personality*. Monterey, CA: Brooks / Cole Publishing Co.

Schaeffer, L. (2002). The Leadership Journey. *Harvard Business Review*, Oct.

Skinner, B. F. (1974). *About Behaviorism*. New York: Knopf.

Stephenson, C. (2004). Rebuilding Trust: The Integral Role of Leadership in Fostering Values, Honesty, And Vision. *Ivey Business Journal*. London: Jan./Feb.

Stogdill, R. (1948). Personal Factors Associated With Leadership: A Survey of the Literature. *Journal of Psychology*, 25, 35-71.

Stogdill, R. (1974). *Handbook of Leadership*. New York: The Free Press.

Zaleznik, A. (1977). Managers & Leaders: Are they different? *Harvard Business Review*, May-June.

Chapter 2

Buckingham, M. & Clifton, D. (2001). *Now Discover Your Strengths*. Free Press.

Personnel Decisions International, (2000). *The Successful Manager's Handbook*. Personnel Decisions International Corporation.

Schein, E. (1992). *Organizational Culture and Leadership*. Jossey-Bass. Inc.

Chapter 3

Bandura, A. (1977). *Social Learning Theory*. Prentice Hall.

La Ganga, M. (1994, May 18). Are There Words that Neither Offend Nor Bore? *Los Angeles Times*.

Leo, J. (1993, Dec. 13). Falling For Sensitivity. *US New & World Report*.

Mallory, J. (1988). *Dress For Success*. Warner Books.

Mayfield, M. & Mayfield, J. (2004). The Effects of Leader Communication on Worker Innovation. *American Business Review*, June, Vol. 22.

Chapter 4

Evered, R. and Selman, J. (1999). Coaching and the Art of Management. *Organizational Dynamic*. Vol. 18.

Lombardo, M. and Eichinger, R. (2000). *For Your Improvement*. Lominger Limited.

Wellins, R. and Rioux, S. (2000). The Growing Pains of Globilizing Human Resources. *Training and Development*, Vol. 54.

Chapter 5

Amabile, T. (1995). *Assessing the Climate for Creativity.* Center For Creative Leadership.

Collins, J. (2001). *Good to Great.* New York: HarperCollins Publishing, Inc.

Denrell, J. (2005). Selection Bias and the Perils of Benchmarking. *Harvard Business Review,* April.

Florida, R. (2004). America's Looming Creativity Crisis. *Harvard Business Review,* Oct.

Gunn, B. (2003). Delegating Decisions. *Strategic Finance,* Jan. Vol. 84.

Herzberg, F. (2002). One More Time: How Do You Motivate Employees? *Harvard Business Review,* Jan.

Hughes, D. (2003). Add Creativity to Your Decisions Processes. *The Journal for Quality and Participation,* Vol. 26.

Livingston, S. (2003). Pygmalion in Management. *Harvard Business Review,* Jan.

Madjar, N., Oldham, G., and Pratt, M. (2002). There's No Place Like Home? The Contributions of Work and Nonwork Creativity Support to Employees' Creative Performance. *Academy of Management Journal,* Aug.

Mangel, M. and Samaniego, F. (1984). Abraham Wald's Work on Aircraft Survivability. *Journal of the American Statistical Association.*

Chapter 6

Bettelheim, B. (1943). Individual and Mass Behavior in Extreme Situations. *Journal of Abnormal and Social Psychology, 34.* 417-452.

Naughton, R. (1975). Motivational Factors of American Prisoners of War Held by the Democratic Republic of Vietnam. *Naval War College Review, 27.* 2-14.

Rahe, R. & Genender, E. (1983). Adaptation to and Recovery From Captivity Stress. *Military Medicine, 148,* 577-585.

Schutz, W. (1966). *Interpersonal Underworld.* Palo Alto, CA: Science and Behavioral Books, Inc.

Schutz, W. (1992). Beyond FIRO-B--Three New Theory-derived Measures— Element B: Behavior, Element F: Feelings, Element S: Self. *Psychological Reports, 70,* 915-937.

Chapter 7

Abrahamson, E. (2000). Change Without Pain. *Harvard Business Review*, Jul./ Aug.

Ahn, M., Adamson, J. & Dombusch, D. (2004). From Leaders to Leadership: Managing Change. *Journal of Leadership & Organizational Studies*, Vol. 10.

Duck, J. (1998). Managing Change: The Art of Balancing. *Harvard Business Review on Change*. Harvard Business School Publishing.

Goss, T., Pascale, R., and Athos, A. (1998). "The Reinvention Roller Coaster: Risking the Present for a Powerful Future." *Harvard Business Review on Change*. Harvard Business School Publishing.

Kegan, R. & Lahey, L. (2001). The Real Reason People Won't Change. *Harvard Business Review*, Nov.

Kotter, J. & Schlesinger, L. (1979). Choosing Strategies for Change. *Harvard Business Review*, March-April.

LaClair, J. & Rao, R. (2002). Helping Employees Embrace Change. *The McKinsey Quarterly*, No. 4.

Martin, K., Quigley, M. & Rogers, S. (2005). Implementing a Learning Management System Globally: An Innovative Change Management Approach. *IBM Systems Journal*, Vol. 44.

Moran, J. & Avergun, A. (1997). Creating Lasting Change. *The TQM Magazine*, Vol. 9.

Pascale, R. & Sternin, J. (2005). Your Company's Secret Change Agents. *Harvard Business Review*, May.

Personnel Decisions International, (2000). *The Successful Manager's Handbook*. Personnel Decisions International Corporation.

Senge, P. (1990). *The Fifth Discipline*. New York: Doubleday.

Schaeffer, R. & Thompson (1992). H. Successful Change Programs Begin With Results. *Harvard Business Review*, Jan.-Feb.

Chapter 8

Argyle, M. (1983). Five Kinds of Small Social Groups, In H. Blumberg, A. Hare, V. Kent & M. Davies (Eds.), *Small Groups and Social Interaction. New York:* John Wiley and Sons, Ltd.

Berman-Rossi, T. (1992). Empowering Groups Through Understanding Stages of Group Development. *Social Work With Groups*, *15*, 239-255.

Bossidy, L. & Charan, R. (2002). *Execution: The Discipline of Getting Things Done*. New York: Crown Publishing Group.

Canary, D. & Sptizberg, B. (1987). Appropriateness and Effectivness Perceptions of Conflict Strategies. *Human Communication Research, 14,* 93-118.

Harrington-Mackin, D. (1994). *The Team Building Tool Kit.* New York: Amacom.

Katz, D. & Kahn, R. (1966). *The Social Psychology of Organizations.* New York: John Wiley & Sons.

Katzenbach, J.R. & Smith, D.K. (1993). *The Wisdom of Teams.* New York: Harper-Collins.

Lencioni, P. (2002). *The Five Dysfunctions of a Team.* San Francisco: Jossey-Bass.

Riley, P., (1994). *The Winner Within: A Life Plan for Team Players.* New York: Berkley Books.

Schutz, W. (1960). *The Interpersonal Underworld.* Palo Alto, CA: Science & Behavior Books Inc.

Senge, P. (1990). *The Fifth Discipline.* New York: Doubleday.

Tubbs, S. (1988). *A Systems Approach to Small Group Interaction.* New York: Random House.

Tuckman, B. (1965). Development Sequence in Small Groups. *Psychological Bulletin, 63,* 384-399.

Von Bertalanffy, L. (1952). *Problems of Life.* London: Watts & Co.

Wellins, R, Byham, W. & Wilson, J. (1991). *Empowered Teams.* San Francisco: Jossey-Bass.

Zajonc, R. (1963). Social Facilitation. *Science, 149,* 269-274.

Zenger, J. (1994). *Leading Teams: Mastering the New Role.* Irwin, IL: Business One.

Vogl-Bauer, S. (1995). Examining Stress in Small Groups. *Small Group Communication.* Madison WI: Wm. C. Brown.

Chapter 9

Bowen, J. (2004). The Dream Team: Staffing Your Organization with Top Notch Players is a Three Part Process. Here's How to Get Started. *Financial Planning.*

Bossidy, L. & Charan, R. (2002). *Execution: The Discipline of Getting Things Done.* New York: Crown Publishing Group..

Collins, J. (2002). *Built To Last.* New York: Harper Business Essentials.

Feiertag, H. (2003). Written Job Descriptions Help to Determine Qualified Applicants. *Hotel and Motel Management*, Vol. 218.

Mornell, P. (1998). *Hiring Smart!* Berkley, CA: Ten Speed Press.

Smart, B. (1999). *Topgrading.* Upper Saddle River, NJ: Prentice Hall Press.

Chapter 10

Breene, T. & Nunes, P. (2005). Balance Alignment and Renewal: Understanding Competitive Essence. *Outlook*, No. 1.

Cohn, J., Khurana, R., & Reeves, L. (2005). Growing Talent as if Your Business Depended on It. *Harvard Business Review*, Sept.-Oct.

Collins, J. (2001). *Good to Great.* New York: HarperCollins Publishers Inc.

Goffee, R. & Jones, G. (2000). Why Should Anyone Be Led By You? *Harvard Business Review,* Sept.-Oct.

Luthans, F., Luthans, K., Hodgetts, R, & Luthans, B. (2002). Positive Approach to Leadership (PAL): Implications For Today's Organizations. *Journal of Leadership Studies*, Vol. 8 No. 2.

Peters, Tom. (2001). Rule #3: Leadership is Confusing as Hell. *Fast Company*, March.

Peterson, S. & Luthans, F. (2003). The Positive Impact and Development of Hopeful Leaders. *Leadership & Organizational Development Journal*, Vol. 24.

ACKNOWLEDGEMENTS

The writing of a book is seldom a solo journey, and certainly this book is no exception. Over the past 30 years, countless clients, students, peers, friends, and family members have provided wonderful grist for this mill.

At the top of the list of people who need to be thanked are the Vietnam Prisoners of War who shared their stories, insights, and experiences to help me understand better what I already knew about leadership and then to challenge me to dig deeper to discover what is truly required to lead others through adversity. I am grateful to the POWs and all the dedicated physicians, technicians, and support staff at the Robert E. Mitchell Prisoner of War Center for allowing me to study with and learn from them. To them, and to all who have served in our military, we owe a debt of gratitude.

Next on the list of those deserving my thanks would be the numerous clients who influenced my journey through our mutual learning and discovery. Special thanks to my construction clients at Alberici, McCarthy Building Company, McBride Homes, Builders Bloc, and Vantage Homes for allowing me to use their stories.

In the food, grocery, and convenience store industries, leaders at Tyson Foods, Price Chopper Groceries, Wallis, and Dierbergs Markets provided invaluable insights about what it takes to be a magnetic boss in industries that are characterized by high turnover.

In addition to my clients, others have encouraged me along the way. Darlene Dudley generously loaned me her laptop when mine failed during a writing trip to South Carolina. Alan Weiss, my mentor, has become an invaluable source of wisdom, and three members of his mentoring group, Pam Harper, Rose Jonas, and Nancy McKay, have joined forces to help me navigate the unfamiliar waters of book production.

Then, there are my readers, supportive people who gave me advice and guidance: Dick Anderegg, Marilyn Davis, Rose Jonas, Craig Nafziger, Angie and Pat Origliasso, and Carol Weisman. A special thanks goes to Linda Eardley for her diligent proofreading.

Finally, I want to thank my family for their ongoing love and encouragement: daughter Angela Origliasso and her husband, Pat, and two children, Michele and Patrick; daughter Sherry and her husband, Jason, and youngest daughter, Laura. They rallied to do what needed to be done so I could travel, work, and write, all elements of turning the idea of retaining top performers into the reality of *The Magnetic Boss*.